TWENTIETH CENTURY VIEWS

The aim of this series is to present the best
in contemporary critical opinion on major
authors, providing a twentieth century perspective on their changing status in an era
of profound revaluation.

Maynard Mack, *Series Editor*
Yale University

NATHANAEL WEST

NATHANAEL WEST

A COLLECTION OF CRITICAL ESSAYS

Edited by

Jay Martin

Prentice-Hall, Inc. *Englewood Cliffs, N.J.*

A SPECTRUM BOOK

Acknowledgment is gratefully made to S. J. Perelman for permission to quote from Nathanael West's *Miss Lonelyhearts*, "Some Notes on *Miss Lonelyhearts*," *A Cool Million*, and *The Day of the Locust*.

10 9 8 7 6 5 4 3 2 1

PRENTICE-HALL INTERNATIONAL, INC. (*London*)
PRENTICE-HALL OF AUSTRALIA, PTY. LTD. (*Sydney*)
PRENTICE-HALL OF CANADA, LTD. (*Toronto*)
PRENTICE-HALL OF INDIA PRIVATE LIMITED (*New Delhi*)
PRENTICE-HALL OF JAPAN, INC. (*Tokyo*)

Contents

To S. J. Perelman
and
In Memory of
Laura Perelman

Introduction

by Jay Martin

Nathanael West's description of the hero of *The Day of the Locust* as "really a very complicated young man with a whole set of personalities, one inside the other like a nest of Chinese boxes," aptly characterizes West himself.

He was born Nathan Weinstein on October 17, 1903 in New York City to Max and Anna Wallenstein Weinstein, who had emigrated to America only a few years earlier from the province of Kovno in Lithuanian Russia. There, his mother's family had been influential and affluent, regarding themselves as part of the enlightened German-Jewish community. In America, West's father, skilled in the building trades, became a highly successful contractor for large apartment buildings in uptown New York and the Bronx. Quite naturally, both parents cherished for their son and their two daughters, Hinda and Laura, the highest hopes for success.

But by heritage and temperament West possessed what Lillian Hellman has called a "dark side to his nature." Edmund Wilson, who knew him well, remarks that he had "a kind of eastern European" suffering and sense of the grotesque, "in common with Gogol and Chagall," and also "a sad, quick Jewish humor," "a quality of imagination which was . . . both Russian and Jewish." Moreover, his heritage was given special shadings by his own dark personality and the conditions and demands of life in America during the first four decades of this century.

He was intelligent and imaginative, and even at an early age his reading was, his sister Laura remembers, "enormous." He often read several books at the same time and was ever recommending books to friends and family. Professional standing through education had been one of the means by which Jews in Russia had been able to escape from the restrictions of the Pale, and education in America seemed to immigrants to provide the clearest path to success. His parents, therefore, presented him regularly with sets of the "standard" authors—

1

Tolstoy, Turgenev, Pushkin, Dostoyevsky, and Chekhov; Dickens, Thackeray, and Shakespeare; Maupassant and Balzac. West himself haunted used bookstores and sent for the catalogues of English booksellers. By the time he reached Brown University in 1922, he knew a strange amalgam of literary tradition: not only such Church Fathers as St. Augustine, but also such modern poets as Eliot and Pound; English writers of the 1890s as well as French symbolists; classical authors like Petronius and Suetonius, but also precious "modern" novelists like Arthur Machen and James Branch Cabell. In all, he decidedly preferred the bizarre and exquisite to the conventional and achieved.

This special emphasis carried over into other activities; very early he responded to the grotesque in any form. His conversation was extraordinary. He collected and told unusual tales, almost always dealing with the odd or unpleasant aspects of whatever interested him at the moment. In particular, he delighted in stories about strange weapons and exotic methods of torture and could describe both in considerable detail. He spoke of cruelty as "something special and distinguishing," and was preoccupied with disease, corruptibility, witchcraft, occultism, and mysticism. From the first he thought, as a friend has said, "in violent terms and in terms of violence."

In all these interests he was clearly creating an identity very different from that which his parents were proposing for him. Matthew Josephson has remarked of his own childhood in New York during this same period: "We might be of mixed English, German, Irish or French ancestry, or, as in my own case, Jewish, yet the prevailing 'Protestant Ethic' of middle-class America seemed to possess all our parents alike. They were anxious and mainly preoccupied with all that was material and useful in 'getting ahead.' " West's parents' hopes, of course, coincided with the American Dream of Success; and they pointed to successful lawyers, doctors, or businessmen as models for his emulation. They moved close to the best schools in New York City and guided their children toward Ivy League colleges.

Bright and capable of conventional success of this kind, West yet resisted all of their plans. The whole issue of success and failure was always to be highly charged for him; he may have felt, as children often do in families where material success is of such importance, that his parents identified him not as a person so much as an instrument of their achievement and thus have unconsciously failed where they most urged him to succeed. In school he read books of his own choice and was frequently absent, busy exploring the rank life of the city. In

June of 1920 he left DeWitt Clinton High School without graduating.
Yet, for his own self-esteem he could not accept failure, even in
conventional areas. He wished to be truly distinguished. "We were
not going to be American peasants," one of his cousins says, "we were
going to be American gentlemen." Through a complicated series of
maneuvers, West contrived to be admitted first to Tufts College, then
to Brown University; in 1924, having passed two years of college work,
he graduated from Brown with a Ph.D. By this time, too, he had
begun to see that if he would not build houses he could make novels.
The craft of construction, which he had learned only partly, he was
transmuting into the art of the novel, where he would be a master.

II

His novels, of course, were the major expressions of the labyrinths
of West's personality. The chief source of his personal complexity lay
in the contrast between his intellectual and emotional life, between
his ability passively to understand experience and his initial lack of
capacity for deeply active involvement in it. Philip Wylie, who met
West in 1925, describes him as a divided person—"thin, restless, discontent, sardonic, homely, and very warm and affectionate under that."
To some of his friends he showed only the sardonic and to others only
the warm and sympathetic aspects of his divided self. In common with
James Joyce and Max Ernst (both of whom he admired) West possessed
a merciless, intellectual humor, which some of his acquaintances saw
as "intellectual brutalism." Certainly he was absolutely intolerant of
pretense and sometimes refused even to talk to people whom he regarded as dull or superficial. To other close friends, like Malcolm
Cowley, however, West appeared truly "soft and vulnerable"—his surface cynicism "a cover-up for a real desire to make contact." Those
people closest to him, like Laura and her husband, S. J. Perelman,
whom West met first at Brown, have movingly described his tenderness
and warmth.

One of the characters in West's first novel describes himself as "on
the side of the intellect against the emotions, on the side of the brain
against the heart." But West's opposing self was ever taking opposite
sides. Robert M. Coates has well summed up the complexities of this
tension. The central principle of West's character, he believes, was "his
immense, sorrowful . . . all-pervasive pessimism. But [Coates adds]
though this colored all his thinking both creatively and critically, it

had no effect on his personality, for he was one of the best companions I have ever known, cheerful, thoughtful, and very flexible in all his personal attitudes."

III

The Dream Life of Balso Snell (1931), West's first novel, was largely the product of his wit, the sardonic side of his personality. Begun as early as 1924 and partly written in Paris, this short novel was not finished until 1930. It is the account of a journey that an American Babbit takes through the anus of the Trojan Horse, and of his encounters there with various forms of deception, pretense, and illusion. West at once set his innocent, innocuous mock-hero upon an investigation into the Western tradition itself. Imaginative, witty, and wildly inventive, this book well expresses the sense of literary internationalism that West shared at this period with his peers. In form it resembles, of course, the short, tight French novella that West and his contemporaries most admired. Many of its themes, too, are closely allied with continental preoccupations. Breton, Picasso, Klee, Joyce and others had experimented with the dream life of man, the nightlife of the soul. Scorning ordinary social values and emphasizing man's interior life, the whole tendency of experimental literature between 1920 and 1930 had been to turn values inside out—to declare the primacy of dreams over acts, of violence over order, of Sade's sexual gospel over that of the churches; of arbitrary over calculated action; and then to announce the superiority of the criminal, insane man, or the clown, over the bourgeois citizen.

West first proposed to take his epigraph for *Balso Snell* from Kurt Schwitters: "anything that the artist expectorates is art." At the last moment, quoting from a character of Marcel Proust's, he changed his epigraph to suggest that life is a journey. But in *Balso Snell* movement is only vagrant wandering, travel only travail. The Trojan Horse hardly suggests epic questing—West called his book in 1924 a "parody" of the Troy story—only the deceitfulness of dreams, and thus of the life which these dreams symbolize. If life is a journey, then, it is a journey through illusion, and the book which describes it is, like Anatole France's *Penguin Island* (a book which West admired), an anatomy of illusion.

In this first novel West at once faced the problems that would occupy all of his fiction: how to satirize illusions when they seem necessary in the modern world, when the future of an illusion seems to be only the proliferation of greater illusions; how to assign guilt in a post-Freudian age when even blame has been rendered difficult; and how to make these conditions tragic when both the need and the guilt for illusions lie in the very nature of man and his world. West understood only tentatively in this book, but with brilliant effect in his others, that he would need to invent new literary forms and attitudes to express, for the modern sensibility, moral indignation without righteousness, and a tragic sense without a vision of redemption.

West was thus to turn his initial lack of capacity for deep personal involvement, the source of his wit, into an extraordinary capacity for compassionate involvement in the life of the masses. His intellectualism would issue into a richly poetic and complex craftsmanship; and his personal vulnerability into deep artistic sympathy.

* * *

Even while West was completing *The Dream Life of Balso Snell* he was pondering the condition of bruised people in the modern world. In 1929, through S. J. Perelman, he happened upon a collection of letters written to the Lonelyhearts column of a Brooklyn newspaper. These, he saw at once, were submerged cries of pain from anonymous, almost archetypal people, despairing and yet hedged by hope for an answer from "The Susan Chesters, the Beatrice Fairfaxes and the Miss Lonelyhearts . . . the priests of twentieth-century America." Deeply moved by the letters, and more and more aware of his own capacities, West worked on his second novel for nearly four years, completing his final draft in November of 1932.

Miss Lonelyhearts (1933) is the tale of a newspaperman who casually takes on the job of giving moral advice. In consequence, however, he poses for himself moral questions that he had, like his fellows, been able before to avoid facing. "Perhaps I can make you understand," this young man tells his fiancée. "Let's start from the beginning. A man is hired to give advice to the readers of a newspaper. The job is a circulation stunt and the whole staff considers it a joke. He welcomes the job, for it might lead to a gossip column, and anyway he's tired of being a leg man. He too considers the job a joke, but after several months at it the joke begins to escape him. He sees that the majority of the letters are profoundly humble pleas for moral and spiritual advice, that they are inarticulate expressions of genuine suffering. He also discovers that his correspondents take him seriously. For the first time in his life, he is forced to examine the values for which he lives.

The examination shows him that he is the victim of the joke and
not its perpetrator."

Doubtless the otherwise unnamed hero, Miss Lonelyhearts, under-
stands his mission in too simplified a fashion, and he is here not so
much summarizing his transformation as crystallizing his own con-
fusions. Still, the novel does move from comedy—the jokes of Shrike—
to an exploration of the archetypes of the "genuine suffering" of both
Miss Lonelyhearts and his correspondents. Perhaps West's own phrase,
"moral satire," best describes the mixed character of this novel. Like
Balso Snell, Miss Lonelyhearts is an anatomy of illusion. But here, the
hero unmasks illusions only to find that people cannot live without
them. He himself is at last appealing only because he commits himself to the greatest of illusions—the personal redemption of the mass.
Yet, though his compulsions and sympathies drive him to the Christ
dream, his intellect drives him from belief in it. He is impaled by his
antagonist, the butcher-bird, Shrike, on the thorns of this dilemma.
West originally intended to imitate the cartoon strip in the structure
of his book, and the novel retains some of the stylized motionless-
movement of the comic strip frame. In a series of episodes Miss
Lonelyhearts moves helplessly from any compulsion to its opposite.
All opposites join in the final episode of the book when, fully accepting the insane illusion that he can win and change the hearts of the
masses, he is shot by the person he wants most to comfort.

W. B. Yeats has asserted that "every writer . . . who has belonged
to the great tradition has had his dream of an impossibly noble life,
and the greater he is the more does it seem to plunge him into some
beautiful or bitter reverie." [1] In *Miss Lonelyhearts* West made an
art-form out of his bitter and comic brooding upon the secret life of
the crowds of people who "moved through the streets with dreamlike
violence." His book shares and combines aspects of both his dreams
of a noble life and his bitterness over its betrayal. Deeply responsive
to the loneliness of the crowd, West was the discoverer and first ex-
plorer of the geography of modern mass solitude.

*   *   *

In his third novel, *A Cool Million* (1934), West explored directly
the American Dream of Success, the myth which lay, as he understood
it, at the heart of so many other frustrations and illusions. Certainly,

[1] William Butler Yeats, "Preface" to the first edition of *The Well of the Saints,*
in *Essays and Introductions* (London: The Macmillan Company, 1961), p. 303.

success had never before seemed so unlikely or hope for personal success so vain as in the early 30s. At the same time that Adolf Hitler was coming to power West was suggesting that there was little essential difference between Horatio Alger's success stories and *Mein Kampf*, and he parodied both in *A Cool Million*. In *Miss Lonelyhearts* he had written generally of the breakdown of faith in modern America; now he wrote of the perversion of the traditional American faith in success.

West's major aesthetic problem in writing *A Cool Million* was to convey the special character of economic and political wish-fulfillment thinking. In an essay printed in this volume I discuss the kind of literary collage that West created from major nineteenth- and twentieth-century expressions of the success-ideal. Influenced by the technique and point-of-view of S. J. Perelman, to whom the book is dedicated, West attempted to reveal the absurdity of the myth of success by confronting it directly with the reality of the 30s. The result is highly ironic. Though the novel is ostensibly, as Perelman has said, the most comic of West's books, as in *Candide* and *Gulliver's Travels*, books which it closely resembles, bitterness and disillusion flow just beneath its comic froth.

From his first three novels West earned only $780. Moreover, after *A Cool Million*, the short stories which he wrote failed to sell, the theatrical enterprises which he planned went unproduced, and the Guggenheim Fellowship for which he applied went to others. In the summer of 1933 he had worked as a junior writer for Columbia Pictures while *Miss Lonelyhearts* was being prepared at Twentieth-Century for film production. In 1935, he returned to Hollywood. During the last five years of his life West labored in the dream factories of Republic, R.K.O., Universal, and Columbia. But unlike F. Scott Fitzgerald and many other writers, he never aspired to make great films. He preferred to work on B- or even C-grade pictures, since these did not touch the sources of the creative energy for his fiction; he regarded movies simply as a source of support.

More important, perhaps, than the money that West made in movies was the material that Hollywood life provided for his fiction. As early as 1933 he formed a plan to write a novel about the subterranean life of the dream capital. In the spring of 1935 he began to collect materials and to sketch out his new book. By choosing with calculation to live near Hollywood Boulevard, West explored a seamy area where dreams, violence, and deception mixed, affecting "the cultists of all sorts, economic as well as religious . . . who can only be stirred by the promise of miracles and then only to violence. . . . a great united

front of screwballs and screwboxes." [2] The frustrated cultists and those
who excited them; victims and victimizers; the starers and the dancers
—these provided the material and form for West's fourth novel, *The
Day of the Locust* (1939).

West gave his novel two opposing curves of development. The first
consists of the story of the relations between the "dancers" and the
"torchbearers," the "super-promisers" and their dupes. The middle-
aged émigrés to California are represented by Homer, the man of the
crowd, and the Hollywood underworld by Faye, Earle, Abe, and
Miguel. Both groups move downward, from desire to frustration and
from discontent to frenzy. The upward curve of development in the
novel occurs in the art of Tod Hackett, a graduate of the Yale School
of Fine Arts who has been hired by National Films to design costumes
and sets. Dissatisfied with the kind of merely illustrative painting
that he had been trained to do and with the masters—Homer and
Ryder—whom he had been taught to admire, Tod attempts to renew
his art by learning the secrets of Hollywood life. He learns to use new
painting techniques of the surreal and grotesque, resembling those of
James Ensor; and he adopts new masters, the painters of mystery and
decay, like Salvator Rosa, Monsu Desiderio, and Alessandro Magnasco.

Certainly, Tod's personality, disintegrating during the novel, inter-
sects the first curve of development: beginning as an illusion-maker,
an employee of a film studio, he is tormented into becoming one of
the frustrated, violent crowd and ends the book as a prophet of mass
violence. But in his meditations on the principles of a modern art
he expresses the upward curve—of understanding and artistic accom-
plishment. William Dean Howells once told Stephen Crane that
through its sharpened perceptions the novel taught "perspective" to
people who could not use their eyes. West used Howells's painterly
conception in his novel. Even as Tod's personality dissolves, his
artistic perception sharpens. For a moment he can express sanity
through aesthetic order, if only by being willing to give himself up to
the ugly, the nightmarish, and the insane.

IV

As West anxiously awaited the appearance of *The Day of the Locust*,
he was compelled to raise for himself the kind of aesthetic questions

---

[2] *The Day of the Locust,* in *The Complete Works of Nathanael West* (New York:
Farrar, Straus and Giroux, Inc., 1957), p. 420.

that had perplexed Tod Hackett. He complained to George Milburn of "how difficult it is to go on making the effort and sacrifices necessary to produce a novel only to find nowhere any just understanding of what the book is about—I mean in the sense of tradition, place in scheme, method, etc., etc." He himself had difficulty in defining his "particular kind of joking," but he groped successfully toward a characterization of his art. "I do consider myself a comic writer," he told Milburn, "perhaps in an older and a much different tradition than Benchley or Frank Sullivan. Humor is another thing; I am not a humorous writer I must admit and have no desire to be one." [3] In trying to place himself in a comic tradition he was perhaps thinking of T. S. Eliot's analysis of Ben Jonson. Certainly Eliot's description of Jonson is equally true for West:

> His type of personality found its relief in something falling under the category of burlesque or farce—though when you are dealing with a *unique* world, like his, these terms fail to appease the desire for definition. It is not, at all events, the farce of Molière: The latter is more analytic, more an intellectual redistribution; it is not defined by the word 'satire.' Jonson poses as a satirist. But satire like Jonson's is great in the end not by hitting off its object, but by creating it; the satire is merely the means which leads to the aesthetic result, the impulse which projects a new world into a new orbit. . . . It is a great caricature, which is beautiful; and a great humour, which is serious.[4]

West's world, however distorted its people may sometimes be, is perfectly clear and complete. If it seems to lack the largeness of Tolstoy's—or of what West himself called "the broad sweep, the big canvas, the shot-gun adjectives, the important people, the significant ideas, the lessons to be taught, the epic Thomas Wolfe, the realistic James Farrell" [5]—still it is precisely drawn to scale, richly complete in its own terms, and boldly direct in its concentrated vision. Malcolm Cowley once remarked that West wrote as if he were sending telegrams to a distant land. His world is a writer's world, as his style is an artist's: his vision and style issue powerfully from his precision and creative intelligence.

[3] Unpublished letter to George Milburn, April 6, 1939; quoted in Jay Martin, *Nathanael West: The Art of His Life* (New York: Farrar, Straus and Giroux, Inc., 1970), p. 335.

[4] T. S. Eliot, "Ben Jonson" (1919), in *Essays on Elizabethan Drama* (New York: Harcourt Brace Jovanovich, Inc., 1956), p. 80.

[5] Unpublished letter to F. Scott Fitzgerald, April 5, 1939; quoted in Martin, *Nathanael West*, p. 334.

At the present time, West is popularly known as the progenitor of the black humor of the 60s. But his permanent reputation will hardly rest upon this. West never attempted to correct society through satire or abandon it through irony; he held no dark mirror up to life. But he created a permanently true artistic vision, unaffected by alterations in the actual world. His works remain parallel to our lives, brilliant instruments through which we can measure and understand the crucial issues of our age. In them, West offered no comprehensive criticism of the temporal world; rather, he created a more permanent perspective by which that world, at any time, might be understood and judged. Satirists who construct their own complete worlds, such as Persius, Rabelais, Johnson, and Dickens, are the writers to whom West may most accurately be compared. However our world changes (and, admittedly, since West's death it has come to resemble more and more the chaotic world of his fiction), his art seems likely to possess the same interest and power.

Nathanael West: A Portrait

by S. J. Perelman

Picture to yourself a ruddy-cheeked, stocky sort of chap, dressed in loose tweeds, a stubby briar in his teeth, with a firm yet humorous mouth, generous to a fault, everready for a flagon of nut-brown ale with his cronies, possessing the courage of a lion and the tenderness of a woman, an intellectual vagabond, a connoisseur of first editions, fine wines, and beautiful women, well above six feet in height and distinguished for his pallor, a dweller in the world of books, his keen grey eyes belying the sensual lip, equally at home browsing through the bookstalls along the Paris quais and rubbing elbows in the smart literary salons of the Faubourg St. Honore, a rigid abstainer and non-smoker, living entirely on dehydrated fruits, cereals, and nuts, rarely leaving his monastic cell, an intimate of Cocteau, Picasso, Joyce and Lincoln Kirstein, a dead shot, a past master of the foils, dictating his novels, plays, poems, short stories, epigrams, aphorisms, and sayings to a corps of secretaries at lightning speed, an expert judge of horseflesh, the owner of a model farm equipped with the latest dairy devices—a man as sharp as a razor, as dull as a hoe, as clean as a whistle, as tough as nails, as white as snow, as black as the raven's wing, and as poor as Job. A man kind and captious, sweet and sour, fat and thin, tall and short, racked with fever, plagued by the locust, beset by witches, hag-ridden, cross-grained, a fun-loving, serious-minded dreamer, visionary and slippered pantaloon. Picture to yourself such a man, I say, and you won't have the faintest idea of Nathanael West.

To begin with, the author of *Miss Lonelyhearts* is only eighteen inches high. He is very sensitive about his stature and only goes out after dark, and then armed with a tiny umbrella with which he beats off cats who try to attack him. Being unable to climb into his bed, which is at least two feet taller than himself, he has been forced to

"Nathanael West: A Portrait" by S. J. Perelman. From *Contempo* 3 (July 25, 1933): 1, 4. Reprinted by permission of the author.

sleep in the lower drawer of a bureau since childhood, and is somewhat savage in consequence. He is meticulously dressed, however, and never goes abroad without his green cloth gloves and neat nankeen breeches. His age is a matter of speculation. He claims to remember the Battle of the Boyne and on a fine night his piping voice may be heard in the glen lifted in the strains of "For She's my Molly-O." Of one thing we can be sure; he was seen by unimpeachable witnesses at Austerlitz, Jena, and Wagram, where he made personal appearances through the courtesy of Milton Fink of Fink & Biesemyer, his agents. What I like about him most is his mouth, a jagged scarlet wound etched against the unforgettable blankness of his face. I love his sudden impish smile, the twinkle of those alert green eyes, and the print of his cloven foot in the shrubbery. I love the curly brown locks cascading down his receding forehead; I love the wind in the willows, the boy in the bush, and the seven against Thebes. I love coffee, I love tea, I love the girls and the girls love me. And I'm going to be a civil engineer when I grow up, no matter WHAT Mamma says.

Nathanael West

by Josephine Herbst

Four short novels, a play, a few random stories, and a handful of
scenarios for Hollywood comprise the totality of the work of Nathanael
West. The novels were published within the space of a single decade,
the '30s. The first novel, *The Dream Life of Balso Snell,* written after
his sojourn in Paris in the '20s, was not published until 1931. The
novels are dark parables embodying West's vision of what it means to be
a human being in this world. There are no heroes. The one heroic
battle is between fighting cocks in *The Day of the Locust.* The only
battle scene, in the same novel, is a sham Waterloo on a collapsing
Hollywood set. Whether they are housewives or whores, Mexicans or
cowboys, Alger boys struggling upward, journalists or would-be actors,
the people in West's novels are all bit players in a violent modern
drama of impersonal collective forces. There are no big shots; no
tycoons; no one can be said to be in the money. The only valid
currency is suffering. The paraphernalia of suffering surrounds the
sufferers and streams from the air. The vibrations surge from irrational
impulses from within, powerful and inexplicable forces from without.
If there is a vision of love it is etched in the acid of what love is
not. If there is courage it is no more than the persistence of human
beings to endure in spite of all.

The horror of this age was in West's nerves, in his blood. This
horror creates a pallid atmosphere in *Miss Lonelyhearts,* a half-light
round men and things. It suggests the lighting of the German ex-
pressionist stage of the '20s, where a single beam could prick from the
dark the coil of a sinister staircase; the ring of iron in the floor betray
the fatal trap door. West felt physically the chaos of his time. Hence
the unparalleled force of his images. This language can be tasted; it
rings in the ears; tingles along the spine. It contains bottomless sadness,

"Nathanael West" by Josephine Herbst. From *Kenyon Review* 23 (1961): 611–30.
Reprinted by permission of the publisher.

mad wit, and a melancholy tenderness. West's pessimism is an absolute
true finding.

Nothing in the work distracts from the astringency of West's central
vision of a world in trouble. The world is not only in deep distress;
its people are captives. Their chains are forged from within; they are
also man-made from without, and man succumbs to a dual fate of
within-without. Man's collaboration with *things*, the paraphernalia
of his suffering, is realized in the metaphor where West's vision takes
effect. When a man smiles, his fat cheeks are "bunched like twin rolls
of smooth pink toilet paper." Miss Lonelyhearts proposes marriage
"to a party dress." Mrs. Doyle's massive hams are like "two enormous
grindstones." Even a bird song in *The Day of the Locust* sounds "like
water dripping on something hollow, the bottom of a silver pot perhaps, then like a stick dragging slowly over the strings of a harp." The
sound of the harp is released not by the bird but by the bottom of the
pot. A slow spring rain changes "the dusty tar roofs to a shiny patent
leather." The sky is "canvas colored and ill-stretched." Skyscrapers
"menace" a little park. Faye Greener's beautiful body in *The Day* is a
thing; she uses it or withholds it as a potentially valuable acquisition.
The tension between the visible and invisible, between the perceived
and the apprehended, is set up and releasd by grim humor, out-
rageous paradox, by the use of an idiom which serves as the "connection" between the world of things and the dream world, between the
nightmare and the vaguely aspiring. But the combination of all the
devices adds up to more than bleak pessimism by virtue of an ir-
repressible visionary gaiety that spurts with wry humor in the idiom
and metaphor.

Perhaps no modern writer used to better advantage the concrete
evidence available to him for projecting his own particular vision. The
sense of permanence to be found in West's fiction is paradoxically
achieved by a deep penetration of the present. Though the real content does not spring from the conscious, but from the creative subconscious, the elements dredged up from below are objectified in concrete terms. They can be seen, heard, touched, smelled. The language
has the savage economy of shorthand. The words are alive. They elbow
their way on to the page, gesture, blaze, fade and die. There are no
synthetic syrups in this mixture. The assimilated medium is for the
exteriorization of thought; there is little or no attempt at subjectivism
or generalization.

Humanity in West's novels is about its own business. It is at work
in itself and for itself and the business is botched. West's view of hu-

manity is not a philosophical one; it is more the detached attitude of Joyce's Daedalus who describes Epictetus to the Master of Studies as "an old gentleman who said that the soul is very like a bucketful of water." Forces act upon humanity but by means of humanity. Humanity in West appears to be circling with fatal monotony around an unseen fulcrum. The people in West's fiction are not so much looking for something they have lost as for something they never had and never will have. Their lives are splintered, held together by wisps. The splinters stick into one another's skins, prick, bleed in themselves and into one another. The scenes of violence are prefigured in the constant threat of violence in the very air. The threat is in things and streets and in the beings who await their daily dole of existence within the confinement of circumstances. From Iowa to Los Angeles is no journey; flight does not free them. Nor can they escape from their own skins. Only Miss Lonelyhearts makes a genuine but strangulated attempt; out of emptiness in himself he struggles to feel universal love —the love he cannot feel for a single individual. For the rest there is the triviality of day-by-day, ruptured by sensual floundering, raw fornication, the gesture of wanting, the tedium of waiting. Who feels or inspires imaginative desire? There are no Jeanne Duvals. The beauty of Faye Greener in *The Day* is a waste.

The motive power of West's work from first to last was a fascinated disgust with the processes of the body and an accompanying obsession with physical violence. His virtues, his limitations; his scabrous wit, effective social satire, his compulsion to shock and his lapses into self-pity all spring from the same source. The passionate feeling in this fiction streams from West, not from his individual characters. It animates the inanimate. The helplessness of his individuals to communicate with fellow beings is heightened to nightmare proportions in the gulf of non-communication in which people move like somnambulists. But the inability of the individuals in the novels to communicate is compensated in West by the extreme lucidity of the prose. West's coming to terms with incomprehensible emotional forces is counterbalanced by his own strenuous efforts at rigorous control of language.

West was not ignored during his lifetime nor did he swim against the stream of fashion. *Balso Snell* was so obviously a belated detonation from the '20s that it received little attention. The severity with which he unmasked, exposed, and demolished the falsities enveloping the human being in the three novels to follow *Balso* had no compensating vision. There is no future in West's fiction; no victories, either

within or without. What alienated him from a wide audience in the
'30s was the extreme pessimism of his attitude toward society and its
institutions. It is this nihilistic pessimism, the sense that all institutions
are shams and that the act of love is merely "the incandescence that
precedes being more lonely than ever" that plays a large part in earn-
ing respect for West today. If it is a period when the obvious illusions
have evaporated, it is also one intellectually proud of discarding
"ideals."

Before the second World War, before the hydrogen bomb, or the
Cold War, Nathanael West was dead. He had gone to Paris in the '20s,
had witnessed the depression, the Spanish Civil War, the Moscow
trials, the Munich pact, the Nazi-Soviet pact and had survived intact
through a decade that had killed or reduced to anonymous fragments countless human beings. The decade retired some of his gifted
fellow-writers to neglect or oblivion. Others suffered silence or evolved
in painful mutations to something else. How West's work might have
developed is scarcely a matter of speculation. But in a recent study of
the life and art of Nathanael West,[1] James Light has quoted a letter
from West to his publisher written in the last year of his existence. He
was no longer interested, he wrote, in pessimistic writing; in the
future—and not just because such art sold—he planned to write
simple, warm, and kindly books. Whether he would ever have achieved
writing of this order is questionable. It sounds more like a Westian
joke. The basic nature of the writer was ingrained to a severe critical
vision and the new epoch would hardly have validated his proposed
views. But the man, West, had probably experienced in that final year
his rewarding human experience; he had fallen in love and had
married at last; he was happy. He may have sprung his own personal
trap.

In his *Nathanael West* James Light has given us the fullest account yet to appear in print of the life, and, if it does not give us the
"real" image of the man, who is to say what that was? Did West know?
The tension between the true life, reality as we have felt it, and its
very different outward appearance is peculiarly marked in West and
manifests itself conspicuously in the work. Light has drawn from
every source available to him and the conflicting viewpoints only sub-
stantiate the complexity of West. We learn little about West's forma-
tive years, so important for the evolution of the artist. Most of the information comes from West's fellow students at Brown or from friends

[1] *Nathanael West: An Interpretative Study* by James F. Light. Northwestern
University Press.

and acquaintances of later years. He is described as plain and awkward by some; by others, attractive and graceful. A sense of his conversation, his way of moving, listening, what he read and the ideas he prodded at, used or discarded are put together with admirable clarity and add up to a view of the man as he developed as an artist. *Nathanael West* includes not only a critical examination of the four novels but Light's researches into the little known stories and Hollywood scenarios. The work contains many interesting and well documented details of information—descriptions of the Dadaist and surrealist influences which prevailed as a continuous force in West's fiction; a discussion of the uses he made of his attraction-repulsion complex toward Joyce, Dostoevsky, and Baudelaire.

One of the most rewarding sections in *Nathanael West* deals with an exposition of the methods and influences which governed the writing of *The Dream Life of Balso Snell.* As Light indicates, this early work prefigures the later writing. All the elements to be amplified in the later novels are within the storehouse of this early fantasy. The self-mockery, the blasphemy, the obscenity, the determination to turn the blood and excrement, the suffering and cruelty into a joke are accompanied here as in the later work by the deep sense of personal anguish and the condition of the world.

West's artistic personality matured early and the two years in Paris from 1924 to 1926 were favorable to his innate talents. Perhaps James Light stresses too much West's literary antecedents. There is no doubt of the influence that Joyce, Dostoevsky, and Baudelaire had upon his development as an artist, but what is skimped in this account is the even more potent embracing climate of ideas and feelings. Gertrude Stein's lamentable label of "the lost generation" diminished the actuality. Even the war generation was not "lost" in any metaphysical sense; Hemingway denied the state in later years. Nor were they only "sad, sad young men." West was detached in point of time from the earlier group; his viewpoint that maintained from first to last a sense of detachment was native to him. Undoubtedly it was re-enforced by the temporal situations in which he found his place. But in the '20s no one had to give a rational explanation for going to Europe; mobility was in the blood. The Great War had moved all adventuring, all romance to Europe; in America, as Dreiser had demonstrated, again and again, the artist was up against a wall. Henry James had thought of himself as an "outsider." The young writer hastening to Europe had been indoctrinated by the place names in the war news from France; the Marne, Chateau Thierry, Verdun were no longer dots on a map. The deep pessimism in the youth of that day was counterpoised by a paradoxical quixotic romanticism. Even the Dadaists were romantics in the absoluteness with which they embraced their nihilistic concepts, not with ponderous solemnity but with contagious gaiety. It was an international climate; the Dadaists mingled Roumanians and Bulgarians with Germans, Germans with the French. The great love affair for the American youth of the '20s was a love affair with the world. To get out of the constricting present, away from puritanism, prohibition, away from the groveling role of "outsider," of indifferent victor, of a creditor nation in a world in distress. That youthful generation *knew* that the old world was gone forever; that the apparent stability and material progress of society had rested, like everything human, upon the void. But in America the pretense was that nothing had changed. To get in the vortex, to face up to the stern reality may become an urge, a passionate need, and instinctively, knowingly, the young artists determined to submit to it. It was more a desire to *feel* what was in the world to be felt, than to escape something in America, that impelled the youth of that decade to make their pilgrimage. Whether the experimentations in Europe were in painting or poetry, in the theatre or the blueprints of the new architects, the techniques issued from living wells and promised a green beyond. The young American abroad was looking for the "Not-I" of his homeland, that complementary "other" without which the ground beneath his feet could shake and tremble. Only fools could have disdained the disenchantment of the hour. But despair may also breed elation.

In the '20s, the youthful generation lived in the shadows of the Great War; they walked on earth trembling with the reverberations of the Russian Revolution. Signs in the sky flashed forebodingly, prophetically; they warned, they beckoned. No year, no week in the '20s was like any other; it was all flux and ferment with artistic movements evolving to political positions; political situations breeding tension and fission. The avant garde was diversified, intransigent, revolutionary. One contingent extolled the machine; others saw it as the great neuter, abstracting man. The air was filled with voices, in accord and at war with one another. But basically there was unanimity; *to see* at all cost, to refuse to sink in the trivial mirage of day-by-day. If the youthful generation repudiated the betraying parental institutions, they were jubilant orphans seeking their unafraid ancestors who had dared to go below where the demons breed. The truth was the concrete. Don't deal from the deck of generalities; don't pretend you hold the Queen of Hearts when all you have is a spade or club. Don't brag, don't bluff; that's for the business man out for the fast buck.

This was the intoxicating climate West shared in Paris; its momentum was powerful and contagious. In spite of the crash of 1929, the year West began *Miss Lonelyhearts,* the climate continued to prevail; it carried over in the '30s. It was a prime factor in the élan which carried West through, stimulating his sense of the audacious, shooting out rays to repel, to attract. What was innate in him was solid; he stood apart from his contemporaries; he was also of the company. You can see it in *Balso Snell* in comparison of this work with *Eater of Darkness* by Robert Coates. Coates was published in 1926, five years before *Balso Snell,* and the book bore the imprint of Robert McAlmon's Contact Editions in Paris. McAlmon was an inspired entrepreneur of the arts: half demon, half angelic bird. In a black opera cape, his slim figure darted rather than walked from the night world of Montparnasse to Montmartre. His head held high, his thin cheeks often spotted with a bright flush, his eyes quick and assertive, he acted as a go-between the artistic movements of France and America. Writer, publisher, and friend to young writers, he set himself up to transmute the often untransmutable. In the vein of *Balso Snell,* the *Eater of Darkness* employs the grotesque, hallucination, wild humor. But Coates is by no means so severe in his appraisement of the human situation. Nor is he so detached from the prevailing commitment to sensuous experience as the possibly noble avenue to illumination. The sexual in Coates does not descend to the sexual-grotesque. Mind and matter, spirit and flesh are not remorselessly divided and subdivided as in West. The infernal death-ray machine in *Eater of Darkness* may objectify Coates's vision of a threatening technology and a potential sub-humanity, but it is more hilarious than accusatory. Coates doesn't resort to the scatological in West's terms. But neither was West unique in that respect; the use of such terms and four letter words was almost a compulsive mannerism of the period. "The word," obscene or otherwise, was used not only in revenge for a puritan past but as the bullet to shatter the stale frozen mammoths of trite opinions. The Germans indulged in scatology as fully as the Americans; Brecht could top West in *Baal:* "I see the world in a mellow light; it is God's excrement."

An introductory note to *Eater of Darkness* displays the tone of the persuasive impresario: "Robert Coates's dialectic has sometimes the aspect of a Wills-Lenglen tennis battle, but is also vibrant with sensibility. In this age of curiosity, of excursiveness, of discursiveness, one is impelled by the thoroughness even more than by the virtuosity . . .

he proves that classicism and romanticism, objectivity and subjectivity, debility and relativity, when they are not empty formulae, merely constitute approaches to a quality of livingness which includes and transcends them all." Though the key word is *livingness,* a quality to which both writers aspired, this introductory note could never have been applied to *Balso Snell.* It is too playful. But like every other serious young writer of the era, both West and Coates employed a version of what began to be called "athletic prose." The short declarative sentence, the elimination of flabby rhetoric were not inventions of Hemingway. The impetus which had evolved in a variety of new art forms of the epoch took its more immediate shape among the futurists, both Italian and Russian, as well as in the cubist forebears of the surrealists. The Italian manifestoes of 1906, the Russian "Slap in the Face of Public Taste" of 1912, aimed at the gleeful demolition of the old for the sake of the innovating new, and predated Dadaism. In carrying destructiveness to its absolute emptiness, Dadaism had petered out in abstractions. But shortly before West came to Paris, the movement had detonated to surrealism. Both Dadaism and surrealism were undoubtedly potent liberating antecedents for West.

West's deviations from the surrealists are significant. He was with them in pursuing the reality which lies beyond what we call real. He shared—with limitations—the revolutionary element in surrealism which was twofold: it was a revolt of the psyche, against the authority of reason; it was also an appeal to reason to liberate man from his oppressors—family, church, fatherland, and boss. In their utter rejection of the whole conception of bourgeois living for the sake of the mystical idea—*le merveilleux*—the surrealists faced a dilemma. The genii in their Pantheon were Freud *and* Hegel. Pulsing for infinity, in aching concord with impossibilities, the surrealists made a universe always diminishing. Hegel rescued them from gross inwardness; their conception of the human soul evolving like everything else in nature gave a dynamic role to man in the universe. The conflicting tensions between events and internal pressures transformed Breton's homemade formula *Changez la vie!* to Aragon's Marxist position: *Change the world.*

West never ventured beyond the accusatory. More in the vein of Diderot or Stendhal he accepted man as he found him. The one loophole in West's condemned universe that admits a possible ameliorative vision is in *Miss Lonelyhearts.* In its Westian setting, Miss Lonelyhearts' vision of Christ is among the company of the surrealist impossibilities.

Doubtless the clue to the unique quality in the fiction of Nathanael West lies more in what he recoiled from than in what he embraced, but face to face with the man who was also the artist he radiated more of what he liked than what he rejected. In the early fall of 1932, when William Carlos Williams urged John Herrmann and myself to "look up young West," we drove straight from Rutherford to the Hotel Sutton in Manhattan to find him. This tall slim young man with the warm handclasp and infectious smile was the author of *Balso Snell*, and it was no surprise. His composure, his quick repartee, his sudden silences, resounding like a pebble dropped into a well, suggested the complexities, the contraries to be found in the work. He could hand you a drink with the grace of someone offering you a rose; could stand at ease, listening, with the aristocratic air of detached attachment. He could flash and blaze; then, suddenly, you were looking at the opaque figure of a man gone dumpy, thick, who might be brooding behind a cash register in a small shop on a dull day.

We three had dinner together that night in West's hotel and talked as though we had been the oldest of friends. The little magazines of the '20s, published abroad, provided the contiguity for us all. By 1930 they had faded; *transition* was gone; *The Little Review, This Quarter* had folded. Ford Madox Ford's *transatlantic* had given up earlier; the American *Dial*, a more sedate cousin to the intransigeants, had ceased in 1929. *Secession, Broom,* Pound's *Exile* were out or on the way. We had been indoctrinated by the infectious internationalism of the epoch; what went on in Berlin, Rome, Paris, or Moscow was news from home.

The material for the new young writers, however, was not foreign but strictly indigenous. Edward Dahlberg had written *Bottom Dogs* in Brussels; its introduction was by D. H. Lawrence; its content, both in matter and idiom, was pure American. Published in 1930, it preceded by five years *A Cool Million* in exposing the underbelly of the American dream; there was nothing soft about that belly; it was cinder-hardened, work-grimed, flayed yet vulnerable. Dahlberg's anti-hero never achieves even the communion of the rabble horde in *A Cool Million*; a lone individualist, he attempts to dislocate the implacable materiality of his situation, but he is a piece of that materiality, its bone and marrow, experiencing no more than a simple and frightening "being there." The heavy weight of *things* pressed hard upon both Dahlberg and West; the response of each was expressed in reliance upon a unique and flexible use of words for the articulation of the inarticulate. West's affinity with the Faulkner of *As I Lay Dying,* also a publication of 1930, rests in the sense of the comic which both writers used to invest their submerged characters with a crackling livingness. None of these writers uses intellectuals as characters; any attempt to deal with abstractions issues only in the concrete; there are not even any young Nicks up in Michigan. They carry the work of words to a sub-level where non-communicating man is the most lost of the lost; where objects warn, threaten, or console. In the year that gave the Nobel Prize to Sinclair Lewis, the books of both Faulkner and Dahlberg were remaindered. But for the intransigent youth of the '20s, Lewis had never been anywhere except in limbo.

The public and the work of the new young writers were far apart. But, behind the wall, a sympathetic telepathic connection made an in-world for the "outsiders" that was viable. Letters, meetings, chance encounters identified one of the "elected" Unelect. The proposal to drink *Bruderschaft* upon a first acquaintance was not an empty gesture; it indicated apprehension of a longed-for brotherhood. It was a period when impulse was not literary fiction but actual. On the impulse we urged West to come with us to our place in Bucks County the following day. He had confided that he had been working on the book to be called *Miss Lonelyhearts* for three years; later he divulged that he had been carrying in his pocket a marriage license to wed his fiancée for the same length of time. It was delirious autumn and for three days we barely slept. We walked through fields of tall grass, plucked the antlered horns of red sumac, talked of Pushkin for whom autumn had been the creative season. We drank Pennsylvania bootleg rye and homemade red wine; read aloud Carl Sternheim's *A Pair of Underdrawers,* recited poems by Hans Arp, "the trap drummer," and Schwitters' *Revolution in Revon.*

John Herrmann had an autographed copy of George Grosz's *Ecce Homo*; he had known the artist in Germany. We opened the big volume flat on the table, poring over the grotesque comics of the violent Berlin world. We spoke of his *Christ in a Gas Mask,* which had been banned in Germany. Grosz's vision of Christ was of the universal common soldier martyred in the Great War; he himself had been a pacifist who had feigned insanity to avoid induction. The love Miss Lonelyhearts yearns for in his vision of Christ has a similar source; its roots are in humanity, not in a definitive God-seeking. But West's new novel had already taken its final shape before he came to the country where he was shortly to engage a room in an old hotel to complete the work. Taunted with, "If autumn could be the great creative season for Pushkin, why not for you?" he had decided to ask for leave-of-absence from the Hotel Sutton, had picked up our challenge to finish the book, *now or never.*

A comparison of the chapter called "Miss Lonelyhearts on a Field Trip," as it appeared in the magazine *Contact* for October 1932, with the final version, indicates the minute but important particulars which West picked at to the last moment. The extreme tensions in West, which he sought to resolve in his prose, make for finicky writing. Compared with *Bottom Dogs* or *As I Lay Dying* there is a delicate precision in *Miss Lonelyhearts* paradoxical to his violent material. His method may be apprehended in a comparison of the two versions. For instance, he changes "junk that had been made precious by memory" to "junk that memory had made precious." He adds an occasional telling phrase. In "Well, how's the drunkard: Goldsmith asked." he turns the period to a comma, adds, "imitating Shrike." In the sentence "He fastened his eyes on two disembodied genitals copulating" he strikes out "copulating," doubtless at the publisher's insistence. He alters "poppa" to the more American "papa." But the most significant changes are in the names. In this scene Miss Lonelyhearts encounters the fatal Doyles; the wife who will betray him to the husband; the husband who will deny Miss Lonelyhearts his Christ-like role. The *Contact* version gives the name of Mrs. Doyle's child as Mary. West wisely alters it to Lucy. Doyle is called Martin in *Contact*; Martin becomes the more significant Peter, the disciple who denied. At the end of this chapter, when Miss Lonelyhearts has capitulated to the overpowering Mrs. Doyle, the sentence in *Contact* reads: "She rewarded him with a kiss, then dragged him limping to the bed." West cut "limping" as too obvious an identification of the psychic cripple, Miss Lonelyhearts, with the physical cripple, Doyle.

West's belated revision of the key names, Mary and Peter, as well as other interior evidence, indicate that his conception of the role of Miss Lonelyhearts as a seeker of Christ evolved more from the impulse to find love within humanity than to find God. James Light asserts categorically that West understood Christ and his teachings as Dostoevsky did; he substantiates his claim by a letter West once wrote stating his conviction that the survival of humanity depended upon its acceptance of the Christian ideals of Dostoevsky. But exactly what is meant by "Christian ideals"? You might say that Dostoevsky saw all mankind caught in eternal conflict with what he defined as the law of the ego and the law of self-sacrifice. Deeply aware of the duality of man's nature, agonized by inner conflicts, Dostoevsky saw man on earth aspiring toward an ideal in opposition to his nature; this ideal was no less than bringing his egoism in love as a sacrifice to mankind or another creature. For Dostoevsky there was only one sin: failure to fulfill the positive and ultimate ethical ideal of free sacrifice of the individual. Dostoevsky never knew the calm faith or smooth-flowing love that he constantly calls for in his books. He wanted faith; but a demonic lucidity kept him at the edge of grace. He questioned himself and the sacred texts and discussed instead of accepting dogma. The religious impulse in Dostoevsky fused with social-political ideas of his period; the *Underground Man* may be seen as a rebuttal to the rational-egotism of Cherneyshevsky, who voiced the aspirations of the social revolutionaries of the period. But Dostoevsky vetoed the Socialist ideal as the logical extension of the worship of Baal initiated by Western capitalism; he refused to believe that we sacrifice our lives for logical proofs, or even material well-being: "It is for a living internal spiritual image with which well-being is linked, or for the truth of our own nature, or for a dim presentiment of a future vital image for which a logical deduction has respectfully opened the door."

His superior penetration into moral, metaphysical, and aesthetic problems did not prevent Dostoevsky's political views from being the less Chimerical and Utopian. His views of the role of the Russian muzhik are messianic and sentimentalized; in America the social-revolutionaries of the '30s were to sentimentalize "the worker."

West sentimentalized no one. In his detachment from the prevailing climate of the '30s he refrained from Utopias but he shared the emotions which could produce a version of the free sacrifice of individuals in Silone's *Fontamara* and Malraux's *Man's Fate.* But West's concern for the world stopped with a delineation of its dire predicament; in the severity of his vision he condemns mankind to a deterministic cycle as completely as the adherents of economic-determinism but without their futuristic goal.

The movement in *Miss Lonelyhearts* from imprisoned within to the prison without brings no victory. The will to love humanity is ironically in vain. Miss Lonelyhearts is made definitely concrete; he is the son of a Baptist minister to whom, as a boy, the vision of a snake arises when he shouts the name of Christ. In Miss Lonelyhearts the suppression of the forbidden leads to disgust and guilt. His cloven chin in combination with his high puritan brow and thin nose are the concrete representations of his duality. His longing for a unified self pushes up from the subconscious; he takes the Christ from the cross of his crucifix and nails him, a lone man, on the wall. The cross is the symbol of the eternal duality in man from which Miss Lonelyhearts seeks escape. He is an empty bottle in a world of doorknobs. As he approaches his mystical vision he becomes the insensate rock; the eddies swirl around him. When he proposes to Betty she is "a party dress" and he behaves in the male version of a Hemingway heroine: "He was just what the party dress wanted him to be: simple and sweet, whimsical and poetic, a trifle collegiate yet very masculine." His seeking takes secular form; he does not pore over Holy Writ but studies the words of Dostoevsky's Father Zossima about loving humanity.

This sad moralist was by intention a satirist, but he offers no positive idea; if his novels signal "beware," they present no prospect either within the self or in the world beyond an engulfing moment. What he shared with Dostoevsky was a horror of the emptiness of sterile intellect, a hatred of dogma. He shared a Dostoevskian compassion which prevented him from creating any actual villains in his vision of a world ruled by the villainy of the little.

Light tends to reflect more of the climate of the '50s than of the era in which West lived, felt, created. The penitents of that earlier decade have poured lava over some of the living elements which should once again be seen in their original verdure to make sense of the time and the place. No matter the eventualities—no matter the errors—the conflicting ideologies the tragedies. To see what West used and discarded one must return to the *Then* and strip away the *Now*. There is nothing false about *Light's* documentation of the '30s. He gives the words but does not actually evoke the tune. The opportunities for self-sacrifice and devotion to common causes for the sake of humanity, under various banners—mistaken or not—were multiple. The period produced genuine anonymous heroic individuals battling for more than the fast buck, for more than their own fate. But in *A Cool Million* West sees only the ignoble, only the deluded. He signals to a danger which never materialized in the terms he envisioned. What finally did emerge, on yet more threatening upper levels, is far more complex, far more obscure, more universally ominous than anything he prognosticated in concrete terms. But his sense of the Laocoön-strangulating embrace of material processes upon human material is acute and prophetic.

The value of West's fiction arises from the authenticity with which he used his own within in conjunction with his own without. In comparison to other writers of the period his experience in life seems to have been oddly limited. Compared to the rovers who submitted to multiple jobs—the early Dahlberg and Faulkner descended to the menial—the orbit in which he moved is restricted to college, two years

in Paris, successive managerships of two hotels, two years in a house
in the country, then Hollywood as the final stage. He traveled rarely
and with revulsion. Inspired by descriptions John Herrmann and I had
given him of the Key West and Mexico, he ventured but was not en-
chanted. In his first summer in Hollywood he wrote:

> This place is just like Asbury Park, New Jersey. The same stucco houses,
> women in pajamas, delicatessen stores, etc. There is nothing to do,
> except tennis, golf or the movies. The trip out was terrible. They ought
> to sell Kansas to the Armenians. It was 112 in the car as we passed
> through the cornbelt. The desert is full of tin cans and old tires. The
> Mississippi that I saw is nowhere as beautiful as the Hudson and the
> Colorado doesn't compare with the Delaware. The climate out here
> makes me feel peculiar. I get very sleepy about 9 o'clock and must go
> to bed by 11. The sun gave me a frightful headache and I have to wear
> smoked glasses all the time. In other words, phooey on Cal. Another
> thing, this stuff about easy work is all wrong. My hours are from 10
> in the morning to six at night with a full day of Saturday. They gave me
> a job to do five minutes after I sat down in my office—a scenario about
> a Beauty parlor—and I'm expected to turn out pages and pages a day.
> There's no fooling here. All the writers sit in cells in a row and the min-
> ute a typewriter stops someone pokes his head in the door to see if you
> are thinking. Otherwise, it's like the hotel business.

He had gone to Hollywood after *Miss Lonelyhearts* was published in
the spring of 1933; it had not sold enough to enable him to write in
the house he had bought in our neighborhood with his sister Laura
and her husband, S. J. Perelman. His trip to Hollywood was in their
company and his intimate life in all the years I knew him was closely
tied to their lives. They had an apartment in the Hotel Sutton when
West was its manager; the three made trips together, shared an apartment in Hollywood, and were always in close touch. The "fiancée"
never materialized into a wife. Though he wasn't a man without
women, none of his friends mentions any romantic love affair in Light's
account of him. He had closer ties to his family than any of the other
young writers of the period whom I knew. In that respect, as well as in
other aspects, he was totally unlike Hemingway. He loved to hunt
but his manner in the woods and fields was always slightly disengaged;
he had no code; you could accompany him without being obligated to
display skill. There was an abstaining restraint in West which led him
to accept the limitations of his existence and, in submitting to them,
to pass to his own beyond. He could go to Hollywood without suc-
cumbing to it.

Some of his flights of fancy involving possible escapes from the economic trap were as fantastic as his inventions. On a later engagement in Hollywood he wrote asking if our notion of getting a boat to sail around the world wasn't possible. It was the summer of 1933; he expected to be back in the country soon where he "intended to stay until he starved or was put out." Then he added: "But there's a trip I would like to take. That's to the Indies in the boat we talked about. Instead of buying a boat couldn't we charter one for six months. I should think that you could get a 6 or 7 thousand dollar boat for a thousand dollars. But I wouldn't be able to start until about xmas and then I don't know what year. But in all seriousness is such a trip possible."

It wasn't. We, as well as he, were in deeper difficulties than any of us would admit. But West came back to the country he loved, began a careful study of the Alger books, and, imitating their style, wrote *A Cool Million.* It's possible that the Grosz cartoon of a boy rummaging in a garbage can—with the slogan "You were right, Mother, the first million is the hardest"—may have contributed to the title. When it did not sell, when it received little attention in a year when readers were swimming in the syrup of *Goodbye, Mr. Chips* and when the gifted novel, *Call It Sleep,* by Henry Roth went without any appreciable notice, West grimly returned to Hollywood.

In the late fall of 1935 he wrote that he had a long hard-luck story to tell me when we met. "I'll be back soon after the new year tolls its melancholy knell. I've written a book, but I'm fed up on books and it's going to be the last even if it sells two thousand copies, even twenty-five hundred. Jo, we've got to turn to the theatre: It's a bonanza, an El Dorado, a Golden Hind, a, a . . . Or maybe a job in a library. But I don't think I'd like working in a library. Otherwise, nothing. I'm just waiting for my turn to be smuggled across the line via the underground R. R. to Canada. Harriet Beecher Stowe and the Bronson Alcotts have interested themselves in my case and It won't be long now. Up Abolition! The new slogan is CHARLES A. ARTHUR RIDES AGAIN."

The reference to being smuggled to Canada was an oblique smack at Sinclair Lewis' *It Can't Happen Here* where the hero is transported across the line ahead of vigilantes. But Hollywood was West's *without* from then on; his *within* he furnished himself. Sometimes in the woods he loved; sometimes shooting quail; sometimes wild doves. He transformed his own without of Hollywood in terms of his own within, just as he had translated the Hotel Sutton in terms of *Miss Lonely-*

hearts, when he wrote his final novel, *The Day of the Locust.* Once more he displayed rare originality and fantastic imaginative power in his treatment of his theme.

The finest passages are those in which violence, and particularly mob violence, is described and analyzed, and in which he makes a real attempt to give universal significance to his personal agonies, to his own deep fears.

Through the Hole in the Mundane Millstone

by *Nathanael West*

Three men read *The Dream Life of Balso Snell* and, having in mind perhaps an older story involving Picasso, exclaimed in rapid succession:

"Almost as funny as the Venus de Milo!"

"As funny as the Venus de Milo!"

"Funnier than the Venus de Milo!"

We quote this incident not only because the book is extremely funny, but also because the hero of it, Balso Snell, a lyric poet by trade, often indulges in violent exclamations. The examples that follow have been chosen at random from the text:

"O Anon! O Onan!"

"O Beer! O Meyerbeer! O Bach! O Offenbach!"

"O Constipation of Desire! O Diarrhoea of Love!"

English humor has always prided itself on being good natured and in the best of taste. This fact makes it difficult to compare N. W. West with other comic writers, as he is vicious, mean, ugly, obscene and insane. We feel with good cause. For much too long has the whimsical, family-joke (tongue in cheek, hand over heart, good-fellows all) dominated our literature. With the French, however, West can well be compared. In his use of the violently disassociated, the dehumanized marvelous, the deliberately criminal and imbecilic, he is much like Guillaume Apollinaire, Jarry, Ribemont Dessaignes, Raymond Roussel, and certain of the surrealistes.

Nevertheless, the mechanism used—an "anywhere out of the world" device—makes a formal comparison with Lewis Carroll possible. Just as Alice escapes through the looking glass, Balso Snell escapes the real world by entering the Wooden Horse of the Greeks which he finds in the tall grass surrounding the walls of Troy; inside he hires a

"Through the Hole in the Mundane Millstone" by Nathanael West. This piece was published as an advertisement for *The Dream Life of Balso Snell*, by West's publishers, Moss and Kamin, in 1931.

philosophic guide who insists on discussing the nature of art. After a violent argument, Balso eludes him only to run into Maloney the Areopagite who is attempting to crucify himself with thumb tacks. Maloney tells Balso that he is writing a life of Saint Puce. This saint is a flea who built a church in the armpit of our Lord, a church "whose walls are the flesh of Christ, whose windows are rose with the blood of Christ." After Maloney, he meets John Raskolnikov Gilson, the twelve year old murderer of an idiot, and Miss McGeeney, a school teacher who is writing the life of Samuel Perkins, a man who can smell the strength of iron or even the principles involved in an isosceles triangle.

It becomes apparent to Balso that the intestine of the horse is inhabited solely by authors in search of an audience. Disgusted, he attempts to get out but is tricked into listening to other tales. All of these tales are elephantine close-ups of various literary positions and their technical methods; close-ups that make Kurt Schwitters' definition, *"Tout ce'que l'artiste crache, c'est l'art"* [1] seem like an understatement.

[1] ["Anything the artist expectorates is art." —Ed.]

A Picaresque Apprenticeship:
Nathanael West's *The Dream Life of Balso Snell*
and *A Cool Million*

by David D. Galloway

During his own lifetime Nathanael West received little of the serious critical attention for which he consistently hungered. Now, almost a quarter-century after his death, West's literary reputation stands appreciably higher than many of his more prolific contemporaries, and the assiduousness of his followers amounts to a kind of cultism. While West spoke more directly and prophetically of America's delusions and contradictions than even his most perceptive friends realized, the message of his four curiously different novels has found its most sympathetic reception in a post-war generation bombarded by the absurd hyperbole of Madison Avenue and the fear of personal extinction. West saw the seeds of disillusionment and contradiction sown in the American image, had the vision to recognize their relevance far beyond the tempests in political teapots to which many of his friends sacrificed their creative energy, and maintained a comic perspective which causes his anger and despair to emerge with a timeliness characteristic of that art which on the primary level manages to embrace the timeless.

Despite the increasing scholarly attention to which West's novels have been subjected, both *The Dream Life of Balso Snell* and *A Cool Million* rest in a critical limbo, hardly more understood today than they were in West's own time. Neither of these novels displays the richness of composition of *Miss Lonelyhearts* or *The Day of the*

"A Picaresque Apprenticeship: Nathanael West's *The Dream Life of Balso Snell* and *A Cool Million*" by David D. Galloway. From *Wisconsin Studies in Contemporary Literature* 5 (Summer, 1964): 110–26. © 1964 by the Regents of the University of Wisconsin. Reprinted by permission of the publisher.

Locust, for they reveal West at a nearly neurotic point of artistic isolation, and their polemical tone recalls the worst products of the cult of violence of the 1930's. It is, however, this very lack of restraint or control which establishes their value for any study of West's literary significance; in these novels, with their contrived picaresque structures, West's themes, techniques, and influences reveal themselves in raw form. West's style developed and deepened through the writing of these books, and in them the reader can observe the artist as he tries the range of his own comic voice.

Published by an avant-garde Paris firm in 1932, *The Dream Life of Balso Snell* was the direct result of West's impressionable visit to Paris, where for a few years he was able to escape what he had come to regard as the paralyzing commercialism of his own family. Only five hundred copies of the book were printed, and its sole distinction, a partial reprint in the satiric little magazine *Americana,* was at best a dubious one. However, in this first novel West defined his "particular kind of joking," a definition essential to any close analysis of his work:[1]

> An intelligent man finds it easy to laugh at himself but his laughter is not sincere if it is thorough. If I could be Hamlet 'neath this jester's motley, the role would be tolerable. But I always find it necessary to burlesque the mystery of feeling at its source; I must laugh at myself, and if the laugh is "bitter," I must laugh at the laugh. The ritual of feeling demands burlesque and, whether the burlesque is successful or not, a laugh. . . .   (27)

In *Balso Snell,* West introduced his readers to the eccentric, the mystic, the pervert, the crippled, and the disillusioned who were to be credibly presented as major players in his later novels. The themes of cheating, distorted reality, and the Dostoevskian paradox of good and evil occur throughout the book, although they emerge in self-conscious references and images. In the absurdly tweedy figure of Miss McGeeney West first suggests the sterility of modern woman and the failure of sexual gratification. Balso embraces her violently before realizing that she is "a middle-aged woman dressed in a mannish suit and wearing horn-rimmed glasses" (32). Miss Farkis, the bookstore clerk in *Miss Lonelyhearts,* is the direct literary descendant of the mannish schoolteacher in *Balso Snell:* she has "long legs, thick ankles, big hands, a powerful body, a slender neck and childish face

---

[1] All references to West's work are to the collected edition, *The Complete Works of Nathanael West* (New York, 1957).

made tiny by a man's haircut" (72). The most effective and controlled description of the defeminized modern woman, however, occurs in *The Day of the Locust,* where Faye Greener is described as "a tall girl with wide straight shoulders and long, sword-like legs" (270). West's thoughts about society and its continuously intensifying frustrations did not change after the writing of *Balso Snell,* but they concentrated and matured.

As introduction to *Balso Snell,* West quotes from Bergotte that, "After all, my dear fellow, life . . . is a journey." Employing the picaresque technique in his first novel, West satirizes the classic myth of "revelation" which the technique has traditionally illustrated. Balso, the itinerant hero, begins his journey by entering the anus of the Trojan Horse, but unlike Odysseus, Dante and Ishmael, there is no discovery of ultimate truth awaiting him at the end of his voyage. The mucus that clings to the intestines of the Trojan Horse is not the "delicious mollifier" the whale sperm becomes for Ishmael; it is simply mucus, and Balso moves through the rupture-hung interior without direction. Virgil served Dante as a rational guide through the mysteries of purgatory, and Sancho Panza maintained a contact with reality against which his master's illusions assumed their tragi-comic significance, but in the innards of the Trojan Horse there are no guides. An impatient little man with "Tours" embroidered on his cap accosts Balso in the lower intestine, but his talk of reality, studded with the philosopher's jargon of "eaches, everys, anys, and eithers" is unbearable, and Balso continues without his aid.

The Trojan Horse is Balso's world, and like its Homeric predecessor it represents evasion and deceit. For West the modern world is no more honest in the dreams it offers man than the Trojan Horse had been in the dreams of peace with which it tempted the besieged citizens of Troy. The horse as a symbol of sham reappears in *A Cool Million* in Sylvanus Snodgrasse's fatuous panegyrics and in the grotesque rubber figure at the bottom of Claude Estee's swimming pool in *The Day of the Locust.* West knows the misery which exists in his world, and he knows also that "Men have always fought their misery with dreams" (115), that they live, therefore, in a world of distortion not unlike Balso's.

Balso Snell journeys into the dream world of the self in a classic effort to assess his own personality. He approaches religious mysticism, sexual expression, and literary detachment in a manner that foreshadows the agonized gropings of Miss Lonelyhearts. Balso's "Song of Roundness" and his preoccupation with circles both reflect and parody his craving for unity, the kind of wholeness he hoped to find by entering the "Anus Mirabilis":

> Round as the Anus
> Of a Bronze Horse
> Or the Tender Buttons
> Used by Horses for Ani
>
> On the Wheels of His Car
> Ringed Round with Brass
> Clamour the Seraphim
> Tongues of Our Lord
>
> Full Ringing Round
> As the Belly of Silenus
> Giotto Painter of Perfect Circles
> Goes . . . One Motion Round
>
> Round and Full
> Round and Full as
> A Brimming Goblet
> The Dew-Loaded Navel
> Of Mary
> Of Mary Our Mother
>
> Round and Ringing Full
> As the Mouth of a Brimming Goblet
> The Rust-Laden Holes
> In Our Lord's Feet
> Entertain the Jew-Driven Nails. (4)

Like Miss Lonelyhearts' "almost insane sensitiveness to order," Balso's song is the result of his desire to find order in the world. To complete his search successfully, Balso must reconcile man's spiritual and material desires, but he is the archetype of the materialist who can only recognize good in "the Grand Central Station, or the Yale Bowl, or the Holland Tunnel, or the New Madison Square Garden" (6). As a practical man, Balso thinks that Christ is morbid. While his guide's raptures over the beauty of a swollen Doric prostate gland are clearly absurd, Balso's dismissal of the "atrophied pile" represents a deadening literal-mindedness which West frequently condemned; in the miracle of birth Balso imagines ". . . only old Doctor Haasenschweitz who wore rubber gloves and carried a towel over his arm like a waiter" (55). As a journey of self-reconciliation, the visit to the innards of the wooden horse is a failure, for Balso flees the complexities of self which he meets along the way and is unwilling to reconcile other types of intelligence to his own materialistic point of view. In Balso we see developing the bitter cynicism of Shrike, the managing editor of the New York *Post-Dispatch* in *Miss Lonelyhearts.*

It was in large part as a rebellion against materialism that West had visited Paris; at the time he arrived the Dadaists (Masson, Breton, Tristan Tzara, and the other "official" members of the group) were beginning their experiments with super-real ideas. There was an immediate attraction for West in the aim of the early surrealist movement to dispose of the flagrant contradictions between the dream and the waking life. The surrealists showed West a style through which he could express his own inner conflicts. Like those early experimenters, West realized the impossibility of destroying a hostile reality, and therefore chose to ridicule it. The surrealist technique was to prove particularly effective in making mathematically flat characters seem more substantial and in lifting his material above the commonplaces of social protest. In *Balso Snell* West echoed the methods of the new fantastic art through the diary of John R. Gilson: "I acquired the habit of extravagant thought. I now convert everything into fantastic entertainment and the extraordinary has become an obsession. . . ." (27) West never adopted the social and political goals of the surrealists, and he could not accept their premise of art for art's sake. It was their method which appealed to him, both as a gesture against reality and, conversely, as a way of conveying the pointlessness of the irrational dream-life. The strange, incongruous paintings of the surrealists—like Dali's "Debris of an Automobile Giving Birth to a Blind Horse Eating a Telephone"—seemed to crystallize American culture. A drugstore was for West the most characteristic American institution, a fantastic *collage* outlining the comic delineations of the national state of mind in rows of douche bags, egg beaters, vitamin pills, muscle relievers, baby bottles, and athletic supporters. There is an obvious stylistic correlation between this image and the one which Lautréamont evoked in *Maldoror:* "Beau comme . . . la rencontre fortuite sur une table de dissection d'une machine à coudre et d'un parapluie." [2]

The early surrealists sought the kind of intellectual abandon which destroyed "real" relationships and created the super-real impressions which they felt necessary to consider philosophical problems

---

[2] Quoted in Herbert Read, ed., *Surrealism* (London, 1936), p. 191. ["As beautiful as . . . the casual encounter of a sewing machine and an umbrella on an operating table."—Ed.]

objectively. Yielding to the revolutionary tactics of Rimbaud and Lautréamont which encouraged ridicule and negation of reality, surrealistic expression inclined increasingly toward the new depths of the sub- and pre-conscious recently probed by Freud. With the surrealists, West feared that

> As a man grows up, he evolves into a well-regulated automaton, whose comportment is determined by positive material considerations and by shrewd intellectual reasoning. At the same time, a hopeless mediocrity has settled somehow upon all his actions and desires. . . . Sublime inspiration has been so well expunged from his life that the average adult seems condemned to run endlessly in a maddening circle of dullness.[3]

Sharing many of their basic precepts, West was fascinated with the surrealists' intention to use "the imagination, the fantastic, to carry man outside himself." [4]

The painter Max Ernst, an important molding force in the surrealist movement, was a favorite of West; *Miss Lonelyhearts* is perhaps dedicated to him, and in any event West's novels owe a great deal to his spirit.[5] Ernst's artistic technique has had an obvious influence on such descriptive passages as "houses that are protuberances on the skin of the streets," "like the gums of false teeth are the signs imploring you to enter the game paths lit by iron flowers," and "She choked the rose with butter and cake crumbs, soiling the crispness of its dainty petals with gravy and cheese" (32, 57).

By surrealistically coupling traditional Christian illusions with vulgar physical images, West shows the incongruities of the real and the imaginary life: the communion ritual is likened to an insect's munching the flesh in Christ's hairy armpit. If a satisfactory reality is attainable, West argues, it cannot be discovered through popular Christian mythology. Maloney's biography of St. Puce the Flea is a burlesque of the mystery writings through which this mythology has traditionally

---

[3] George Lemaître, *From Cubism to Surrealism in French Literature* (Cambridge, 1941), p. 195.
[4] Read, p. 246.
[5] Shortly after West's literary star began to rise in the early 1950's, more than one "Max" stepped forward to reveal his identity as the dedicatee, but their claims seem spurious. Ernst's artistic hold on West was great at the time he wrote *Miss Lonelyhearts*, but West's own father perhaps has greater claim to the dedication. West was generally detached from the members of his family and noticeably unemotional about them. The exceptions were his sister Laura and his father, whom West always lovingly called "Max." (The dedicatee was West's father. [Ed].)

been expressed. West, like Dostoevsky and William James, does not dispute the aims of popular Christianity, but the methods which it employs. The distorted ritualism which Maloney represents as he struggles to crucify himself with thumbtacks is illustrative of the unending psychomacy which results from Christian practices. Confronted with the self-flagellation of Maloney, Balso advises, " 'Don't be morbid. Take your eyes off your navel. Take your head from under your armpit. Stop sniffing mortality. Play games. Don't read so many books. Take cold showers. Eat more meat' " (13). Although Balso's cynical practicality is not the answer to man's spiritual needs, Christianity nevertheless appears to be another of man's comically puny attempts to impose order on an irrational world.

West was remorseless in exposing the dreams by which man strives to escape the violence and emptiness of life, and *Balso Snell* is a catalogue of the delusions which were to be the subjects of his later work—Christianity, the success dream, artistic detachment, the innocence of childhood, the return to nature, and political idealism. Miss Lonelyhearts, as Balso Snell's successor, runs the full gamut of these delusions. In the opening paragraph of *Miss Lonelyhearts* published in *Contempo*, the little magazine which West for a short while edited with William Carlos Williams, he sounded tragically the various methods the lonelyhearts columnist was to consider in his efforts to avoid the frustration and debased sensuality of society. Miss Lonelyhearts is described sitting at his desk in the *Evening Hawk* building: "Although the street is walled at both ends, he has a Bible in one hand and a philosophy book in the other. In his lap are travel, art, seed, and gun catalogues."[6] Shrike attacks all the forms of escape which these books represent in the symbolically titled chapter, "Miss Lonelyhearts in the dismal swamp." As he exhausts traditional escape methods, Miss Lonelyhearts turns increasingly toward self-torture as a release from his guilt feelings. He removes a figure of Christ from its crucifix and nails it to his bedroom wall with large spikes. This form of self-flagellation, growing out of his increasing identity with Christ, develops explicitly the theme of masochistic Messianism first introduced in Maloney the Areopagite. At first Miss Lonelyhearts strives to resist what Shrike calls the "Christ complex," but he eliminates all other avenues of escape until, overwhelmed by the desire to aid his desperate correspondents, he finds himself "capable of dreaming the Christ dream" (115).

[6] Nathanael West, "Miss Lonelyhearts in the Dismal Swamp," *Contempo*, July 5, 1932, p. 1.

Miss Lonelyhearts' self-flagellation is like the onanistic, compulsive masochism of Dostoevsky, especially as reflected in "Notes from Underground." Dostoevsky's influence on West's work is never so obvious as in the "Crime Journal" of John "Raskolnikov" Gilson, the adolescent underground man whom Balso meets in the horse's interior. Through this diary West is able to suggest that even the idyllic state of childhood has been blighted, although his fascination with the pre-sexual (or, at least, the innocently sexual) world of childhood inspires one of the most sympathetic *vignettes* in his writing. The passage in which Miss Lonelyhearts dreamily recalls his younger sister owes a debt both to West's devotion to his sister Laura and to Natasha's dance in *War and Peace*: "She had never danced before. She danced gravely and carefully, a simple dance yet formal. . . . As Miss Lonelyhearts stood at the bar, swaying slightly to the remembered music, he thought of children dancing. Square replacing oblong and being replaced by circle. Every child, everywhere; in the whole world there was not one child who was not gravely, sweetly dancing" (84). While swaying to this remembered music, Miss Lonelyhearts brushes against a man drinking beer; the man punches him in the mouth. The vision of childhood innocence thus emerges as another of the dreams with which adults torture themselves. Adore Loomis, the child-star-to-be in *The Day of the Locust,* is a vicious, mechanized robot. " 'He thinks,' " his mother apologizes to Tod Hackett and Homer Simpson, " 'he's the Frankenstein monster' " (363).

Christianity is only one of the dreams which cheat modern man, although, as West demonstrates in *Miss Lonelyhearts,* it is the most remorseless of all deceits. The erotic pleasures derived from cheap novels and from the movies, the success myth, social pretense—all represent attempts to flee from the world of reality. Life as West sees it has become a farcical masquerade whose players have long since forgotten their original identities. Gilson's "Crime Journal" describes the killing of an idiot by an insane young man; the idiot "did not have a skull on the top of his neck, only a face; his head was all face—a face without side, back, or top, like a mask" (18). American society appeared to be a travesty performed by masks, and to try to depict that life in terms of conventional realism was impossible for West, just as it proved impossible to use realism as a method for communicating life in Hollywood in *The Day of the Locust.*

Like Swift, West distrusted the very pattern of life, and he found the same impossibility of adjusting to the discrepancies between man's ideals and his accomplishments. West realized, with Swift, that the purpose of satire is to ridicule what one is to demolish, although he did not consistently recognize that the ingredient of humor is essential to effective satire. Horace's "Ridiculum acri fortius et melius magnas plerumque secat res" was one of Swift's favorite texts, and West's technique is its twentieth-century counterpart. When John Gilson wishes to insult bourgeois audiences who feign an arty intellectualism, he suggests an insulting play for one of their art theatres. In the event they should fail to grasp the point of the play, "the ceiling of the theatre will be made to open and cover the occupants with tons of excrement" (31).

West believed that modern society, like Balso Snell in the horse's interior, moved without direction, and this concept is the essence of his vision of man's comic nature. In the rebellion against his own society, the satirist is often eyed with suspicion and disfavor. Thus, readers have made a ready identification of West with the "cultured fiend" in *Balso*, who rages, " 'I was one of those "great despisers" whom Nietzsche loved because "they are the great adorers, they are the arrows of longing for the opposite shore" ' " (20). West was, indeed, a great despiser, and he repeatedly satirized the things he despised; however, the objects of his satire were not men themselves, but the masks which men wore. Violent satire is not congruous with beauty; it is distorted and soured, and the moral it teaches is unpleasant. It is, therefore, frequently misread.

Balso Snell is typical of the intellectual games of blind man's buff which amused café habituées in the 1920's and provided fodder for the little magazines in which West's Montparnasse friends aspired to publish. Much of the novel's vulgarity is obviously intended to shock, and some of it seems to have been conceived with no more serious purpose. *Balso Snell* is a private protest that awaits definition in broader social terms; it is an artist's sounding-board, and from it West obviously learned a great deal. He had hoped that his first novel could be more than a literary exercise, that it might make an effective attack on artiness and superficiality. But because he attacked these subjects with such vindictiveness, and because he threw out conventional plot structure and character development while substituting no alternative literary pattern, *Balso Snell* became one with the very qualities of pretentiousness which it satirized. It is not as a satirist that West achieved artistic success; *A Cool Million*, which satirizes the Alger myth, succeeds at all only because it does not advocate political alternatives. As a humorist who approaches the levels of comic poetry in *Miss Lonelyhearts* and *The Day of the Locust*, West

succeeds as an author because he is not attacking, but *reflecting* a side-
tracked world of sorrow and despair, and because there satire is only a
narrative device, and not his sole method. Though he is intensely involved in the problems which *Miss Lonelyhearts* and *The Day of the
Locust* represent, West is able to see life and human progress as a
prankster's deceit of cosmic—not earthly—proportions.

If the bitterness of *The Dream Life of Balso Snell* is largely intellectual jingoism, the bitterness of *Miss Lonelyhearts* is very real. As
the Depression deepened, West's job as a hotel manager gave him a
significant vantage point; he watched the lobby of Kenmore Hall (and
later the Sutton) fill with unwanted men and women who deluded
themselves with the synthetic dreams of cheap pulp magazines and the
violent excitements of the tabloids. Despite West's greater and more
real anger, *Miss Lonelyhearts* demonstrates a cultivated perspective and
control which would perhaps not have been possible unless West had
first vented his anger in *Balso Snell*; but the generally poor critical
reception of *Miss Lonelyhearts,* published a few weeks before Liveright
declared bankruptcy, disillusioned West, and his anger again gained
the upper hand in *A Cool Million.*

In a letter written to Josephine Herbst in 1932, Nathanael West
commented that his next novel would describe "The breakdown of
the American dream. I'm doing it satirically, of course. I'm re-writing
the Horatio Alger myth—from barge boy to president or from shirt-
sleeves to shirt-sleeves in one generation." [7] West dedicated *A Cool
Million* to S. J. Perelman, and he was consciously imitating certain
characteristics of the style of his financially successful brother-in-law.
Perelman's humor, while often resembling that of a vaudeville joke-
smith, is most obviously characterized by the isolation and fanciful
elaboration of commonplace phenomena in American life. The use
of slap-stick and the isolation of the folklore of *Ragged Dick* and
Tattered Tom in *A Cool Million* resulted in a book reminiscent of
Perelman, but far less artistically successful than West's other novels.
The distinctive prose style which West created is inflated by mock-
heroic language and flawed by limiting topical references. The social
impulses which he attacks are still illusion, and the outcome of illusion
is still physical or spiritual dismantling, but in concentrating his attack
within the sphere of capitalist legend, West created a distinctively
political novel. The book succeeded at all only because West, though
politically angry, managed never to lose his temper.

[7] Letter from Nathanael West to Josephine Herbst, May 31, 1932.

Only a few critics recognized in *A Cool Million* the warning that the inevitable outcome of the frustration of the success dream was the growth of Fascism. Jack Conroy, the proletarian novelist, bought and circulated dozens of copies of the novel among his friends. West reflected several years after its unsuccessful reception that he felt the novel had failed because it was premature in its examination of the possibility of a Fascist America. Shagpoke Whipple's "Leather Shirts" precede Berzelius Windrip's "Minute Men" by more than a year, and that time was sufficient to give Sinclair Lewis's *It Can't Happen Here* a considerably more attentive audience. Despite the relatively early date of his warnings, West did not predict Fascism any more than he had predicted the failure of subjective religious expression. The atmosphere in which he wrote was charged with Fascist warnings, and he merely reflected the growing unrest of labor and urban middle-class groups, whose discontent is summarized in Whipple's speech to Lem: " 'I blame Wall Street and the international bankers. . . . My boy, when we get out of here, there will be two enemies undermining the country which we must fight with tooth and nail. These two arch-enemies of the American Spirit, the spirit of fair play and open competition, are Wall Street and the Communists' " (172). Only the occasional emergence of West's peculiar humor and the absence of Utopian idealism distinguish *A Cool Million* from the other novels of class struggle and economic collapse which were characteristics of the 1930's.

A vital corollary to the Alger myth in American society has been the canard of rugged individualism embodied in such stereotypes of the frontier settler as the swaggering backwoods hero, a type firmly ensconced in American literature by the Southwestern humorists of the nineteenth century. Davy Crockett is the epitome of the rugged frontier hero; in *The Comic Tradition in America*, Kenneth S. Lynn observes that ". . . Crockett had become such a colossal figure in the American imagination that the greatest writer of the age could compare him to a hero of Greek mythology and mean it not only as a joke, but as a serious statement about democratic heroism." Lynn also notes the "sickening violence and appalling cruelty" that often characterized Southwestern humor.[8] West mocked the vernacular braggartism of this native type in the buckskin-clad Pike County man who boasts, " 'I kin whip my weight in wildcats, am a match for a dozen Injuns to oncet,

[8] Kenneth S. Lynn, ed., *The Comic Tradition in America* (New York, 1958), pp. 166, 164.

and can tackle a lion without flinchin'.'" (223) This representative of frontier democracy eats all the food in Whipple's camp, shoots Jake Raven through the chest, and rapes Betty.

A Cool Million, like *The Dream Life of Balso Snell*, utilizes the technique of the picaresque novel. "Lemuel" Pitkin's peccadilloes suggest the demoralizing wanderings of Lemuel Gulliver, and Pitkin's loss of eye, scalp, thumb, and leg makes him a kind of modern-day Candide; but he is not even given the option of rejecting an El Dorado, although for part of his erratic career he does prospect for gold. Balso Snell's journey takes the form of a monotonous circularity, and the psychological voyage of Miss Lonelyhearts ends at an unsatisfactory Calvary. Lemuel Pitkin, in pursuit of the the myth of progress, leaves his snug home on the Rat River only to meet an assassin's bullet at a Fascist convention. Like the stumbling journey of Miss Lonelyhearts, Lemuel's is a quest for certainty and security which ends in death. The mob, for its part, ludicrously makes a hero of "the American boy." Addressing a youth convention that is celebrating Pitkin's Birthday, Mr. Whipple says that " '. . . a thousand years hence no story, no tragedy, no epic poem will be filled with greater wonder, or be followed by mankind with deeper feeling, than that which tells of the life and death of Lemuel Pitkin' " (255). The obvious superficiality of such hero worship demonstrates the warped public consciousness of a nation propelled into elaborate inconsequence as an escape from the realities of frustration and decay. Lemuel's martyrdom is an extenuation of the self-congratulatory national outlook which canonized Davy Crockett and his preposterous braggadocio.

Like Miss Lonelyhearts, Lem is often frustrated by his inability to help those around him. Thus, with a bear trap biting into his leg, he watches helplessly as the Pike man tears off Betty's underwear. Lem lay weltering in a pool of his own blood as "In no way disturbed, the Missourian went coolly about his nefarious business and soon accomplished his purpose" (230). Lemuel trusts in the success myth as Miss Lonelyhearts comes to trust in the Christ myth, and both are defeated by their unquestioning faith. In a scene which predicts his own dismantling, Lem shakes hands with the bully Tom Baxter after a fist fight:

> Lem gave his hand in return without fear that there might be craft in the bully's offer of friendship. The former was a fair-dealing lad himself and he thought that everyone was the same. However, no sooner did Baxter have a hold of his hand than he jerked the poor boy into his embrace and squeezed him insensible.   (154)

While Lemuel's frustration and betrayed confidence involve none of the complexity of Miss Lonelyhearts' psychological frustration, they reflect a cultural naiveté which seemed to West to involve potential danger of almost unparalleled dimensions.

In all West's work there is a fascination with violence that is related to Dostoevsky's concentration on the distorted and the painful, but that also has distinct counterparts in the American literary tradition. The dismantling of Lemuel Pitkin creates a tortuous situation which is reminiscent of Poe and is perhaps traceable to what Melville cited as "that Calvinistic sense of Innate Depravity and Original Sin, from whose visitation, in some shape or other, no freely thinking mind is ever free." [9] The exaggerated sensitivities of Hawthorne, Melville, and Poe cannot be dismissed as possible influences on West's work. Reflecting most strongly the "black" characteristics of American literature, Poe's method as described by Harry Levin is strikingly similar to the techniques which West employs: ". . . the ludicrous heightened into the grotesque, the fearful colored into the horrible, the witty exaggerated into the burlesque, the singular wrought out into the strange and mystical." [10] Poe and West shared the ability to create a nightmarish atmosphere which has strong roots in the anguished fancies of Ann Radcliff and Horace Walpole. While Poe believed that the lyric poem was the most appropriate vehicle for demonstrating the nightmare of life, West felt that the short novel could better accomplish that purpose. "Lyric novels," he argued, "can be written according to Poe's definition of a lyric poem. The short novel is a distinct form especially fitted for use in this country." [11]

The balloon-like dialogue of *A Cool Million* is characteristic of Perelman and reminiscent of the style with which West had experimented in *Miss Lonelyhearts*, a book he had once considered giving the subtitle, "a novel in the form of a comic strip." Although for *Miss Lonelyhearts* West largely abandoned the concept of balloon-like speeches which he had originally intended to use, he nevertheless "retained some of the comic-strip technique." [12] It is tempting to compare West's methods to the startling and grotesque details associated with many popular comic-strips, but his first three novels preceded the horror-and-violence publications inaugurated by "Detective Com-

[9] Herman Melville, "Hawthorne and His Mosses," in *The Shock of Recognition, I*, ed. Edmund Wilson (New York, 1955), p. 192.

[10] Harry Levin, *The Power of Blackness* (New York, 1958), p. 134.

[11] Nathanael West, "Some Notes on Miss L.," *Contempo*, May 15, 1933, p. 1.

[12] *Ibid.*

ics" in 1937. The part of the comic-strip technique which West utilized in *Miss Lonelyhearts* and parodied in *A Cool Million* was the cartoonist's method of showing his characters in a series of pictures, each of which is complete in itself, but forms part of a longer story. Like the enclosed frames in a comic-strip, *Miss Lonelyhearts* is built of a series of boxes through which the action of the novel flows: a newspaper office, a park Delehanty's speakeasy, Miss Lonelyhearts' apartment, an Italian cellar, Betty's apartment, the El Gaucho club, Shrike's apartment, a Connecticut farm, and the Doyles' apartment. The boxes are held together by the passage through them of a character in whom the reader has a vital interest. "Each chapter," West wrote, "instead of going forward in time, also goes backwards, forwards, up and down in space like a picture." [13] This illogical and inverted movement is rescued from the chaos which characterized *Balso Snell* by its relation to specific and detailed "action boxes." The effect lacks the straightline development of a comic-strip, but holds the reader's interest by making him see rather than merely sense intellectual disorder.

A Cool Million is interspersed with purposely hackneyed sentiments like " 'One day, heads will roll in the sand, bearded and unbearded alike' " (222). Despite the author's attempt to escape typing as an artist, however, there are moments when the literary techniques are particularly Westian. The characters Wu Fong and Israel Satinpenny demonstrate the gross incongruities which mark all West's work, and the macaronic decoration of the International Whorehouse recalls the surrealistic drug-store image. Nathanael West's stylistic hallmark is particularly obvious in Chapter 27 of the novel, where Jake Raven's grotesque traveling show is described. As a summary of contradiction, prejudice and injustice, the demonstrations of branding, cheating, torture, and death in The Chamber of American Horrors owes much to a fantastic art of the Dadaists; this debt is particularly obvious in the medical exhibit of the show: "In the center of the principal salon was a gigantic hemorrhoid that was lit from within by electric lights. To give effect of throbbing pain, these lights went on and off" (239).

A number of passages in *A Cool Million* intimate that West wrote it as a conscious and personal intellectual diversion. Lemuel's dismantling by the success myth is not unlike his creator's early critical reception. Lena Haubengrauber, who occupies the "Gaudy Dutch" room in Wu Fong's remodeled whorehouse *à l'américaine*, is a native of Bucks County, Pennsylvania, where West completed *Miss Lonely-*

[13] *Ibid.*

hearts and wrote *A Cool Million*. Lemuel Pitkin rents a room at the Warford House, where West himself lived when he first moved to Bucks County. Despite his own occasional stylistic extravagance, literary pretentiousness was especially distasteful to West, and he mocks it several times in *A Cool Million*, but never so emphatically as in the inflated speech of the poet Snodgrasse: " 'One of the most striking things about his [Lemuel's] heroism is the dominance of the horse motif. This is important because the depression has made all of us Americans conscious of certain spiritual lacks, not the least of which is the symbolic horse' " (183).

At the climax of his career, Lemuel Pitkin is hired as a stooge at the Bijou Theatre, and each night he reaffirms his degrading servitude to the success cult. West introduced his first stooge, or clown, in *Balso Snell*. Beagle Darwin writes to Janey Davenport, the Lepi, that

> The clown is dead; the curtain is down. And when I say clown, I mean you. After all, aren't we all . . . aren't we all clowns? Of course, I know it's old stuff; but what difference does that make? Life *is* a stage; and *we* are all clowns. What is more tragic than the role of a clown? What more filled with all the essentials of great art?—pity and irony.   (50–51)

Beagle Darwin's concept of clownsmanship embraces the same tragic delineations which Aristotle suggested in his comment on the "Spectacle": "Those who . . . put before us that which is merely monstrous and not productive of fear, are wholly out of touch with tragedy." [14]

For West, Lemuel's role is not a tragic one. The author suffers with many of his characters, even if he does so in a curiously indifferent manner, but he suffers less with Lemuel than with his other misguided "fools." It is the content of their dreams, however, which makes the sufferings of Balso Snell, Miss Lonelyhearts, and Tod Hackett ennobling. Even though *A Cool Million* makes a violent critique of the *milieu* in which Lemuel's dream is cultivated, West is so out of sympathy with the character of that dream that he has little sympathy for Lemuel. The "All-American Boy" has been mechanized by materialistic values until he becomes the very incarnation of externality. He permits the world to make of him what it will, and his struggle is not one to rise above the standards of society, but to live by them. It is significant that West chose as subtitle for *A Cool Million* "The Dismantling of Lemuel Pitkin" rather than "The Dismemberment . . . ," for he thus emphasizes Lem's automatonic nature. From his tortuous

---

[14] Aristotle, *De Poetica,* in *The Works of Aristotle* (Oxford, 1924), p. 1453b.

experience with life, the mock-hero emerges with only physical alterations—the grotesque alterations of a circus clown.

The laughter which Lemuel's predicament arouses throughout the novel is like the raucous reaction of the Bijou audience that watches Riley and Robbins batter the stooge over the head with an enormous wooden mallet labeled "The Works." It is a completely different type of laughter from that of *Miss Lonelyhearts* or that aroused by the perpetual clowning of Harry Greener in *The Day of the Locust. A Cool Million* appeals to the reader's intelligence and not to his emotion to recognize the caprice of the Alger myth, and it evokes a burlesque laughter supported by an almost complete anesthesia of the heart. The misfortunes which befall Miss Lonelyhearts and Lemuel Pitkin therefore stimulate responses as inherently different as those aroused by the punishments of Malvolio and Tartuffe.

Violence has created its own context in *A Cool Million,* and the humor of the novel, like that of the animated cartoons, is invariably associated with physical injury. The maiming and brutality of the more violent animated cartoons arouse laughter because the characters are unreal and because, although they are often humanized animals, they lack consciences. Lem's conscience has been replaced by the success myth, and he is the incredulous victim of the jungle of Social Darwinism in which that myth thrives, but his dismantling has a theatrical unreality. Like the animated cartoon characters and circus clowns, who amuse by their affected seriousness and monstrous circumstances, Lem incites no pity and suffers without stimulating in the reader a sense of his pain. To stimulate this sense of the painful does not mean that the clown's actions cease to amuse, as West effectively demonstrated in *Miss Lonelyhearts,* the "Holy Clown." The Holy Clown, however, must lay some human inconsistency that lies deeper than utilitarian attainment and arouse laughter which is related to a primary human emotion if he is to be sympathetic.

Man's sympathy for himself is almost unlimited, but his transfer of that feeling to a fictional character usually demands at least a partial sense of identification; as Bergson has observed, "The comic character is often one with whom, to begin with, our mind, or rather our body, sympathizes." [15] There is nothing in Lemuel Pitkin to stimulate a sympathetic identification with his objectives. He is empty, naive, and a sucker: characteristics which West felt to be deeply ingrained in the American personality; these qualities stimulated West's sense

[15] Henri Bergson, *Laughter* (New York, 1954), p. 194.

of satire rather than his comic point of view. Satire and comedy are not mutually exclusive forms, but they are always in spiritual conflict, for the satirist creates from his own personal dislikes and his response often ends by destroying the balance and "sympathy" which are essential to comedy. West yielded, in *A Cool Million,* to the laughter of the satirist, but he undoubtedly felt that Lemuel's dream deserved no more humane treatment.

Nathanael West wrote his third novel hurriedly in order to meet a publisher's deadline, and his haste undoubtedly contributed to the general stylistic and thematic retrogression of the novel, for it is as flat as the Alger series itself. *A Cool Million* lacks the poetic description, the feeling of economy, and the complexity of expression of *Miss Lonelyhearts* and *The Day of the Locust,* but as an artist's opportunity to detour, practice, and sample, *A Cool Million* bore fruit in *The Day of the Locust* just as *Balso Snell* did in *Miss Lonelyhearts.* Historically, *A Cool Million* is important as the first complete disavowal of the American dream of success and one of the first suggestions of Fascism, but what he had to say about a Fascist America, West said with far greater power in his very unpolitical last novel.

West once referred to *The Dream Life of Balso Snell* as "a protest against writing books"—against distorting literary conventions and academic pretentiousness. This concept of his work reveals West's vital concern over the preservation of the individuality which he felt so severely threatened in twentieth-century America. The interest which William James, Dostoevsky, and the surrealists placed on the importance of the individual obviously had a great deal to do with the attraction they held for West. Even if, as he seems to suggest in *Miss Lonelyhearts,* the battle against mechanization and de-humanization is unsuccessful, the decision to fight is itself a desirable assertion of individuality. Paul Eluard once asked about Baudelaire a question which might be asked about Nathanael West: "Why did he set himself the task of fighting with inflexible rigor against that slavish morality that insures the happiness of supposedly free men?" [16] West answers through Miss Lonelyhearts, " 'All order is doomed, but the battle is worthwhile' " (104). In both *The Dream Life of Balso Snell* and *A Cool Million,* West prepared for that battle.

[16] Henri Ford, ed., *The Mirror of Baudelaire* (Norfolk, Conn., 1942), p. 1.

A New American Writer

by *William Carlos Williams*

No. I don't mean *another* American writer, I mean a *new* one: Nathanael West. When another of the little reviews that appeared in the United States during the last quarter of the century died, I thought it was a shame. But now I think differently. Now I understand that all those little reviews ought by necessity to have a short life, the shorter the better. When they live too long they begin to dry up. But they have had at least one excuse for their existence—they have given birth to at least one excellent writer who would not otherwise have had the means to develop. *Contact* has produced N. West. Now it can die.

The special strength of West, apart from his ability to maneuver words, is that he has taken seriously a theme of great importance so trite that all of us thought there would be no life in it: I mean the terrible moral impoverishment of our youth in the cities.

But to do that he has discovered that the way to treat this theme is to use the dialect natural to such a condition. Since the newspapers are the principal corruptors of all that has value in language, it is with the use of this very journalistic "aspect" and everyday speech that language must be regenerated. West has taken as his material the idiom of the reporters, the tough men of the newspapers, and has counterpointed it with the pathetic letters and emotions of the poor and ignorant city dwellers who write to the newspapers to obtain counsel for their afflictions and poverty.

"A New American Writer" ("Un nuovo scrittore americano") by William Carlos Williams. This article was published in Ezra Pound's literary page of *Il Mare* (XI [January 21, 1931]: 4), translated into Italian by Edmundo Dodsworth. Williams's original version in English has been lost; the article appearing here has been translated back into English by John Erwin and the editor. I am indebted to Donald Gallup, Curator of the American Literature Collection at Yale University for a Xerox of this article. Published by permission of New Directions Publishing Corporation, agents for Mrs. William Carlos Williams. Copyright © 1971 by Florence H. Williams.

After all, what is the urban population made up of? Of seduced and corrupted, nothing more. They have been gathered together so that they may be better exploited, and this is West's material. But no, his "material" is writing itself—he has invented a new manner, he has invented a medium that allows him the full expression of his sentiments in a language which a journalist would recognize. It conveys the real, incredibly dead life of the people and the incredibly dead atmosphere of the book itself and—my God!—we understand what scoundrels we've become in this century. "Don't be deceived" could be West's motto. Don't think yourself literate merely because you write long books and use correct English. Here are the problems, do something with them that will not be a lie. Don't deceive yourself: you don't see because you don't look. These things are there just the same. And if you think you can write poems while you live in a sewer, and at the same time think you're lying in a bed of roses—well, go ahead and be happy!

The cities are rotten and desperate—so is most polite, "literary" literature. So? Nothing much. Only a little review that publishes good material. I don't think that many will find it. It [West's writing] would offend the paying subscribers if it appeared in the large monthly magazines. Which makes one wonder if they will ever let it enter their consciousness.

Some Notes on Violence

by Nathanael West

Is there any meaning in the fact that almost every manuscript we receive has violence for its core? They come to us from every state in the Union, from every type of environment, yet their highest common denominator is violence. It does not necessarily follow that such stories are the easiest to write or that they are the first subjects that young writers attempt. Did not sweetness and light fill the manuscripts rejected, as well as accepted, by the magazines before the war, and Art those immediately after it? We did not start with the ideas of printing tales of violence. We now believe that we would be doing violence by suppressing them.

In America violence is idiomatic. Read our newspapers. To make the front page a murderer has to use his imagination, he also has to use a particularly hideous instrument. Take this morning's paper: FATHER CUTS SON'S THROAT IN BASEBALL ARGUMENT. It appears on an inside page. To make the first page, he should have killed three sons and with a baseball bat instead of a knife. Only liberality and symmetry could have made this daily occurence interesting.

And how must the American writer handle violence? In the July "Criterion," H. S. D. says of a story in our first number that ". . . the thing is incredible, as an event, in spite of its careful detail, simply because such things cannot happen without arousing the strongest emotions in the spectator. (Does not H. S. D. mean, "in the *breast* of the spectator?") Accordingly (the reviewer continues), only an emotional description of the scene will be credible . . . " Credible to an Englishman, yes, perhaps, or to a European, but not to an Amer-

"Some Notes on Violence" by Nathanael West. From *Contact* 1, no. 3 (1932): 132–33. Reprinted by permission of S. J. Perelman.

ican. In America violence is daily. If an "emotional description" in the European sense is given an act of violence, the American should say, "What's all the excitement about," or, "By God, that's a mighty fine piece of writing, that's art."

What is melodramatic in European writing is not necessarily so in American writing. For a European writer to make violence real, he has to do a great deal of careful psychology and sociology. He often needs three hundred pages to motivate one little murder. But not so the American writer. His audience has been prepared and is neither surprised nor shocked if he omits artistic excuses for familiar events. When he reads a little book with eight or ten murders in it, he does not necessarily condemn the book as melodramatic. He is far from the ancient Greeks, and still further from those people who need the naturalism of Zola or the realism of Flaubert to make writing seem "artistically true."

West's Revisions of *Miss Lonelyhearts*

by Carter A. Daniel

Before Nathanael West's *Miss Lonelyhearts* was published in April, 1933, early versions of five chapters had appeared separately in periodicals.[1] A comparison of these early chapters with the versions in the books shows that West made revisions of varying significance on all levels, some throwing light on the basic conception and meaning of the book, and some revealing no more than West's personal preferences in diction and phrasing. An analysis of the revisions is highly rewarding because it helps to clarify the author's aims, some features of his thought, and the technical means by which he solved certain problems of style and structure.

The first of the early chapters (February, 1932) gave "Miss Lonelyhearts" a real name too—Thomas Matlock—but this was an idea which, for good reasons, West soon discarded. The use of a real name eliminates the omnipresent irony of such sentences as "While they held the lamb, Miss Lonelyhearts crouched over it and began to chant" (p. 23),[2] "Miss Lonelyhearts stood at the bar, swaying slightly to the remembered music" p. 37), or "Miss Lonelyhearts lay on his

"West's Revisions of *Miss Lonelyhearts*" by Carter A. Daniel. From *Studies in Bibliography* 16 (1963): 232–43. Reprinted by permission of the author and the publisher.

[1] "Miss Lonelyhearts and the Lamb," *Contact: An American Quarterly Review,* I (February, 1932), 80–85.
"Miss Lonelyhearts and the Dead Pan," *Contact,* I (May, 1932), 13–21.
"Miss Lonelyhearts and the Clean Old Man," *Contact,* I (May, 1932), 22–27.
"Miss Lonelyhearts in the Dismal Swamp," *Contempo,* II (July 5, 1932), 1–2.
"Miss Lonelyhearts on a Field Trip," *Contact,* I (October, 1932), 50–57.

These articles are listed in William White, "Nathanael West: A Bibliography," *Studies in Bibliography,* XI (1958), 207–224. For a discussion of West's connection with the short-lived little magazine *Contact,* see James F. Light, *Nathanael West: An Interpretative Study* (1961), pp. 70–71. *Contempo* was an almost equally short-lived iconoclastic newspaper published in Chapel Hill, North Carolina.

[2] Page numbers not otherwise identified refer to the New Directions edition of *Miss Lonelyhearts,* n.d.

bed fully dressed, just as he had been dumped the night before" (p. 43).
The jolting incongruity in the opening sentence of the final version
was totally lacking in the lifeless original:

February, 1932	April, 1933
Thomas Matlock, the Miss Lonely-hearts of the New York Evening Hawk (Are you in trouble? Do you need advice? Write to Miss Lonely-hearts and she will help you), de-cided to walk from the Hawk Build-ing across the park to Delehanty's speakeasy.	The Miss Lonelyhearts of The New York *Post-Dispatch* (Are-you-in-trou-ble?—Do-you-need-advice?—Write-to-Miss-Lonelyhearts-and-she-will-help-you) sat at his desk and stared at a piece of white cardboard.
	(p. 1)
("Miss Lonelyhearts and the Lamb," p. 80)	

Apparently dissatisfied with the weaknesses incurred by giving Miss
Lonelyhearts a name, West tried in May, 1932, another idea, a first
person narration. With this technique he could easily maintain his
columnist's anonymity and eliminate the disadvantages of the former
method. But now further problems arose from the absence of an ex-
ternal voice which could tell Miss Lonelyhearts' adventures with the
appearance of objectivity. The sardonically matter-of-fact, seemingly
objective narration is a valuable stylistic asset, since to maintain the
continual element of surprise there must be only limited insight into
Miss Lonelyhearts' thoughts. When, for example, as early as the fourth
chapter, Miss Lonelyhearts suddenly plunges his hand into Betty's
dress and feels the nipple of her breast, the reader is sure to be shocked,
or at least surprised; but if Miss Lonelyhearts had been telling his own
story up to this point, West would unavoidably have revealed so much
of the man's character that the episode would even have seemed quite
natural. Moreover, this point of view would have precluded the ending
which West used, wherein Miss Lonelyhearts is shot to death. But
even apart from the ending, first person narration would be largely
unsuitable in a novel which derives most of its impact from the
author's implied ironical judgments of the main character. To use a
first person narration and yet preserve the irony, West would have
had to portray Miss Lonelyhearts as consciously self-critical, which
he clearly is not: though reader and author can plainly see his confusion and incompetence, Miss Lonelyhearts takes himself very seriously, and any change in this view of himself would have affected the
whole general meaning of the book. Finally, the early chapter constantly strains one's credulity simply because a coolly detached first-

person account of so crucial and emotional an experience as Miss Lonelyhearts' seems implausible dramatically:

May, 1932	April, 1933
Backing away from the bar, I collided with a man holding a glass of whiskey. I turned to beg his pardon and received a blow in the mouth. Later I found myself at a table in the backroom, playing with a loose tooth. I wondered why my hat didn't fit, and discovered a lump on the back of my head. I must have fallen. The hurdle was higher than I had thought.	He stepped away from the bar and accidentally collided with a man holding a glass of beer. When he turned to beg the man's pardon, he received a punch in the mouth. Later he found himself at a table in the back room, playing with a loose tooth. He wondered why his hat did not fit and discovered a lump on the back of his head. He must have fallen. The hurdle was higher than he had thought.
My anger swung in large drunken circles. . . .	His anger swung in large drunken circles. . . .
("Miss Lonelyhearts and the Clean Old Man," p. 24)	(pp. 37–38)

After May, 1932, there were no major revisions in the conception of *Miss Lonelyhearts,* but there were still many changes made on a lesser scale. In the chapter published in July, 1932, for example, West experimented with a sort of interior monologue. Instead of having the feature editor Shrike as antagonist in "Miss Lonelyhearts in the Dismal Swamp," a voice in Miss Lonelyhearts' own mind assumes the role. The technique is inconsistent with that of the rest of the book, of course, and it seems very doubtful that Miss Lonelyhearts himself would have had these thoughts. Furthermore, by reapportioning this role to Shrike, West has made him the spokesman for the antagonistic point of view throughout the entire book.[3]

There are also many other revisions which give the work unity and

[3] Prof. Light makes some perceptive comments on the importance of this change, in *Nathanael West,* p. 83.

There is a slight suggestion that the use of the interior monologue may have been the choice of the *Contempo* editors rather than the author. Much of the revision that West ostensibly made later consists only of inserting punctuation, and so, likewise, the interior monologue technique could have been brought about in the first place merely by omitting the original punctuation. Furthermore, there is one "my" in the monologue that seems to refer to an entirely separate person rather than to a part of Miss Lonelyhearts' mind. Still further evidence appears on another page in this same issue of *Contempo:* a letter from an irate contributor claims that his earlier contribution had been greatly changed without permission, and the editors, in a brief reply, rather crassly and fatuously defend their action. In any case, whether West's doing or not, the experiment was an unwise one.

continuity. Each chapter in the novel is a single unit which deals with one incident, whereas some of the previously published chapters were more diffuse. In the earlier version of "Miss Lonelyhearts and the Lamb" the first eight paragraphs told of his preparing to go to Delehanty's, but in the ninth paragraph "He decided against Delehanty's and started home"; in the revision the whole first section was transferred to "Miss Lonelyhearts and the Dead Pan," in which he actually did go to the speakeasy, and thus the dramatic irrelevancy was eliminated. In the original "Miss Lonelyhearts and the Dead Pan" ten of the first twelve paragraphs were devoted to the long letter from Broad-Shoulders; in the revision, this letter is given a chapter to itself ("Miss Lonelyhearts Returns"), leaving the "Dead Pan" chapter to tell solely of the episodes surrounding the evening at Delehanty's. And the original "Miss Lonelyhearts and the Dead Pan" had a serious flaw in its geography: before reading Broad-Shoulders' letter, Miss Lonelyhearts had been in his office; afterwards, without explanation, he was shown in his room; and then he decided to go to Delehanty's. The revised chapter shows him going from his office to the speakeasy and therefore has geographical unity as well as the continuity of plot mentioned above. Finally, the revised "Miss Lonelyhearts in the Dismal Swamp" adds thirty paragraphs, a detailed account of Miss Lonelyhearts' three-day sickness and depression, onto the beginning of the earlier version to provide badly-needed transition between the preceding chapter's account of the Mrs. Doyle incident (which presumably was part of the cause of the depression) and the immediately following heckling by Shrike. Thus three of the five early chapters were altered structurally for the sake of unity.

Many of the revisions helped to make the work unified by providing smooth transitions between chapters or paragraphs or sentences. The original "Miss Lonelyhearts and the Clean Old Man" began bluntly with a new episode, whereas the revised version provides an introductory paragraph to link this chapter with the preceding one, in which Miss Lonelyhearts had been spurned by his fiancee:

May, 1932	April, 1933
I went around to Delehanty's for a drink.	In the street again, Miss Lonelyhearts wondered what to do next. He was too excited to eat and afraid to go home. He felt as though his heart were a bomb, a complicated bomb that would result in a simple explo-
("Miss Lonelyhearts and the Clean Old Man," p. 22)	

sion, wrecking the world without
rocking it.
He decided to go to Delehanty's
for a drink.   (p. 33)

Revision for smoother transition between paragraphs occurred very
frequently. During one of Miss Lonelyhearts' dreams the scene changes
from a theater to a college dormitory, but in only the revised version
is the change accomplished smoothly:

February, 1932	April, 1933
He was back in his college dormitory with Steve Garvey and Jud Hume. ("Miss Lonelyhearts and the Lamb," p. 84)	The scene of the dream changed. He found himself in his college dormitory. With him were Steve Garvey and Jud Hume. (pp. 21–22)

Earlier, in a scene at Delehanty's, Miss Farkis comes in and expresses
her interest in the conversation on religion. Shrike's reaction, originally too sudden either for narrative continuity or for consistency
in the characterization of the cynically calculating, advantage-seeking
feature writer, was carefully anticipated in the revision:

May, 1932	April, 1933
"Get me a drink, and please continue. I'm very much interested in the new thomistic synthesis." "St. Thomas!" Shrike shouted . . . ("Miss Lonelyhearts and the Dead Pan," p. 20)	"Get me a drink and please continue. I'm very much interested in the new thomistic synthesis." This was just the kind of remark for which Shrike was waiting. "St. Thomas!" he shouted. (p. 14)

After leaving Delehanty's on another occasion, Miss Lonelyhearts and
Ned Gates find a "clean old man" in the comfort station of a park;
they take him to a bar, but not to Delehanty's. One additional word
in the revised version makes the narrative more coherent:

May, 1932	April, 1933
Instead of going to Delehanty's . . . ("Miss Lonelyhearts and the Clean Old Man," p. 25)	Instead of going back to Delehanty's . . . (p. 40)

Many passages were revised to make the transition smooth from
sentence to sentence. Generally, the revisions provide information
which was absent in the earlier version and thereby bridge gaps in the

logical order of narration. In Miss Lonelyhearts' dream which was mentioned above, the first image features him on a public platform; the revision adds a sentence to explain how the prayer is connected with the rest of the scene:

February, 1932	April, 1933
. . . he found himself before a micro-phone on the platform of a crowded auditorium. . . . No matter how he struggled his prayer was Shrike's prayer and his voice was the voice of a conductor calling stations. ("Miss Lonelyhearts and the Lamb," p. 83)	. . . he found himself on the stage of a crowded theater. . . . After his act was finished, he tried to lead his audience in prayer. But no matter how hard he struggled, his prayer was one Shrike had taught him and his voice was that of a conductor calling stations. (p. 21)

When he and two of his college classmates see lambs for sale in the farmers' market, they immediately begin planning an exotic adventure; the revision clarifies the previously confused pronouns and provides transition between Jud's idea and Miss Lonelyhearts':

February, 1932	April, 1933
Jud Hume suggested that they buy one and roast it over a fire in the woods. But it was his idea that they should sacrifice it to God before barbecueing it. ("Miss Lonelyhearts and the Lamb," p. 84)	Jud suggested buying one to roast over a fire in the woods. Miss Lonely-hearts agreed, but on the condition that they sacrifice it to God before barbecuing it. (p. 22)

When the ideal of idyllic rural life is proposed as one possible escape from Miss Lonelyhearts' present unresolvable conflict, the revised version furnishes transition between the two contrasted ideas:

July, 1932	April, 1933
. . . the bus takes too long while the subway is crowded so you walk be-hind the enormous millstones of your horse's moist behind . . . ("Miss Lonelyhearts in the Dismal Swamp," p. 2)	The bus takes too long, while the subway is always crowded. So what do you do? So you buy a farm and walk behind your horse's moist be-hind . . . (p. 78)

Just before Miss Lonelyhearts begins his day dream in Delehanty's, the alcohol takes effect and makes him receptive to this kind of reverie; the revised version makes the cause-and-effect relationship clear:

May, 1932

I felt warm and sure. Through the light blue tobacco smoke the mahogany bar shone like wet gold. ("Miss Lonelyhearts and the Clean Old Man," pp. 23–24)

April, 1933

The whisky was good and he felt warm and sure. Through the light-blue tobacco smoke, the mahogany bar shone like wet gold.

(p. 37)

Still another kind of unity is achieved through the removal of irrelevant details and undeveloped themes. Economy and clarity seem to have been West's primary aims in these revisions. He strove to eliminate all but the essential words, symbols, and themes, so that the novel might achieve power through its compactness and its clearness of focus. In the description of Miss Lonelyhearts' room, for example, the revision eliminates an item which does not figure in the story at all and which might mislead the reader and leave him unsatisfied if it were retained:

February, 1932

The walls were bare except for a mirror and an ivory Christ. ("Miss Lonelyhearts and the Lamb," p. 82)

April, 1933

The walls were bare except for an ivory Christ that hung opposite the foot of the bed.

(p. 19)

The description of Hedonism as an alternative to his present way of life was originally an odd paragraph parodying a literary style full of cliches; since this satire interfered with and almost destroyed the meaning of the paragraph, and since it was entirely inconsistent with the other chapters, the revision subordinated it so that now it seems to suggest the triteness of this kind of life:

July, 1932

. . . you make a speech it's in the bag from the start ere the echoes of the starting gun die away headlong for the tape we plunge in the red with too big a nut yet play up play the game although flies in the milk as well as the amber we know full well but seeing as it's better to lie down with a full dog than a dead lion even if the cards are cold marked for emphasis by the hand of fate and you are in a club that won't stand squawks where they deal only one hand and you must sit in so get a run for your

April, 1933

. . . you get to your feet and call for silence in order to explain your philosophy of life. "Life," you say, "is a club where they won't stand for squawks, where they deal you only one hand and you must sit in. So even if the cards are cold and marked by the hand of fate, play up, play up like a gentleman and a sport. Get tanked, grab what's on the buffet, use the girls upstairs, but remember, when you throw box cars, take the curtain like a dead game sport, don't squawk."   (p. 81)

money tank up grab what's on the
buffet and use the girls in the upstairs rooms but when you throw
box cars take it with a dead pan.
        ("Miss Lonelyhearts in the
        Dismal Swamp," p. 2)

In the passage in which the cynics at Delehanty's tell of the female
novelist who started to write a book about "a lot of mugs in a speak,"
the revision eliminates the anticlimactic and irrelevant ending:

May, 1932	April, 1933

Well, the mugs didn't know they were picturesque and thought she was regular until the bartender put them wise. They got her into the back room to teach her a new word and put the boots to her. They didn't let her out for three days. On the third day they sold tickets to niggers. But here's the pay off—she finished the novel.
        ("Miss Lonelyhearts and the Clean Old Man," p. 22)
	Well, the mugs didn't know they were picturesque and thought she was regular until the barkeep put them wise. They got her into the back room to teach her a new word and put the boots to her. They didn't let her out for three days. On the last day they sold tickets to niggers.
	        (p. 34)

And in the earlier version of this same chapter one of the cynics asked,
"What matter if his daily column does not always subscribe to grammar's nice autocracy?" ("Miss Lonelyhearts and the Clean Old Man,"
p. 23). The revised version eliminates this paragraph, since the question
of grammar is one which is entirely irrelevant to the theme of the
novel. These and other similar revisions help *Miss Lonelyhearts* to
achieve its intense focus on the young man's obsessive dilemma.

    Most of the revisions which West made during the year before he
completed his novel were of the kind usually associated with proof-
reading, but they are at least as significant as the changes in conception and structure, by virtue of their contribution to the novel's con-
ciseness. He was clearly a careful and thoughtful proofreader, for
nearly every change is indisputably an improvement, and some of the
most trenchant parts of the novel are the results of these revisions.
Economy was the sole object of some, and of course the impact of the
whole novel is partly attributable to its laconic precision. The aim
of revisions which simplified the syntax, for example, is in perfect accord with the simple, matter-of-fact tone of the narration:

February, 1932   April, 1933
. . . like a spear it pierced him   It pierced him like a spear.
through.   (p. 9)
("Miss Lonelyhearts and the
Lamb," p. 80)

Matlock had given the readers of   He had given his readers many
his column many stones. . . .   stones . . .
("Miss Lonelyhearts and the   (p. 10)
Lamb," p. 81)

Sometimes the revision created a more definite image where the
earlier version had been primarily simply a narration of events:

October, 1932   April, 1933
When he arrived at the obelisk, he   He sat down on a bench near the
sat down on a bench to wait for Mrs. obelisk to wait for Mrs. Doyle.[4]
Doyle.   (p. 64)
("Miss Lonelyhearts on a Field
Trip," p. 53)

Another simple kind of revision was the elimination of repetition. West
was careful to avoid this natural tendency wherever possible:

February, 1932   April, 1933
The decay covering its surface was not The decay that covered the surface
the decay in which life generates.   of the mottled ground was not the
("Miss Lonelyhearts and the   kind in which life generates.
Lamb," p. 80)   (p. 9)

Teach them to pray for their daily   Teach them to pray each morning:
stone: Give us this day our daily   "Give us this day our daily stone."
stone.   (p. 10)
("Miss Lonelyhearts and the
Lamb," p. 81)

No matter how he struggled his   But no matter how hard he struggled,
prayer was Shrike's prayer and his   his prayer was one Shrike had taught
voice was the voice of a conductor   him and his voice was that of a con-
calling stations.   ductor calling stations.
("Miss Lonelyhearts and the   (p. 21)
Lamb," p. 83)

Similar is the elimination of awkward passages and phrases to give
greater coherence and make the work more pictorial, another type of

---

[4] The result of this revision is one example of the "static, pictorial quality" which
Prof. Light shows is an integral part of the novel. See *Nathanael West,* pp. 95–96.

revision which shows West's careful attention to wording. The following change eliminated ambiguity by clarifying the pronoun's antecedent:

February, 1932	April, 1933
Because of its terrible struggles his next stroke went wrong . . . ("Miss Lonelyhearts and the Lamb," p. 84)	He raised the knife again and this time the lamb's violent struggles made him miss altogether. (p. 23)

The following revision reflects syntactically the logical sequence of cause and effect:

May, 1932	April, 1933
I felt as I had felt years before when I had accidentally stepped on a frog. Its spilled guts filled me with pity, but my pity turned to rage when its suffering became real to my senses, and I beat it frantically until it was dead. ("Miss Lonelyhearts and the Clean Old Man," p. 26)	Miss Lonelyhearts felt as he had felt years before, when he had accidentally stepped on a small frog. Its spilled guts had filled him with pity, but when its suffering had become real to his senses, his pity had turned to rage and he had beaten it frantically until it was dead. (p. 41)

In the earlier versions there were a few references too cryptic to be plainly understood. The revisions consisted of rewording or of providing additional information:

May, 1932	April, 1933
At college, and perhaps for a year afterwards, they had believed in literature, had believed in personal expression as a literary end. ("Miss Lonelyhearts and the Clean Old Man," p. 22)	At college, and perhaps for a year afterwards, they had believed in literature, had believed in Beauty and in personal expression as an absolute end. (p. 35)

July, 1932	April, 1933
. . . you are no longer white but golden brown so passing tourists have need of an indignant finger . . . ("Miss Lonelyhearts in the Dismal Swamp," p. 2)	Your body is golden brown like hers, and tourists have need of the indignant finger of the missionary to point you out. (p. 79)

The First Church of Christ Dentist . . . ("Miss Lonelyhearts in the Dismal Swamp," p. 2)	. . . the First Church of Christ Dentist, where He is worshipped as Preventer of Decay. (p. 83)

A great many of the revisions serve to make the finished work more active and vivid than the earlier drafts. Some of the changes were from passive to active voice:

May, 1932
. . . the glasses and bottles with their exploding highlights sounded like a battery of little bells when they were touched together by the bartender. ("Miss Lonelyhearts and the Clean Old Man," p. 24)

April, 1933
The glasses and bottles, their high lights exploding, rang like a battery of little bells when the bartender touched them together.

(p. 37)

October, 1932
. . . junk that had been made precious by memory . . . ("Miss Lonelyhearts on a Field Trip," p. 52)

April, 1933
. . . junk that memory had made precious . . .

(p. 62)

Sometimes the idea became more active through the use of entirely new wording:

May, 1932
Someone suggested raping them. That started a train of stories. ("Miss Lonelyhearts and the Clean Old Man," p. 22)

April, 1933
Then someone started a train of stories by suggesting that what they all needed was a good rape.

(p. 33)

They would go on in this way until they were too drunk to talk. ("Miss Lonelyhearts and the Clean Old Man," p. 22)

[They] would go on telling these stories until they were too drunk to talk. (p. 34)

In other instances West revised the idea itself to make it more lively:

May, 1932
After some pantomime suggesting colorful pageantry, he began again: "Brown Greek manuscripts and mistresses with great smooth marbly limbs." ("Miss Lonelyhearts and the Dead Pan," p. 19)

April, 1933
"To the renaissance!" he kept shouting. "To the renaissance! To the brown Greek manuscripts and mistresses with the great smooth marbly limbs." (p. 12)

Miss Farkis laughed and Shrike looked as though he were going to punch her. ("Miss Lonelyhearts and the Dead Pan," pp. 20–21)

Miss Farkis laughed and Shrike raised his fist as though to strike her.

(p. 15)

Providing additional details to form a more extensive context was one way in which West made the work more vivid:

May, 1932	April, 1933
My sister and I were waiting for father to come home from the church. She was eight years old and I was twelve. I went to the piano and began to play a dance piece by Mozart. I had never voluntarily gone to the piano before. My sister began to dance.	One winter evening, he had been waiting with his little sister for their father to come home from church. She was eight years old then, and he was twelve. Made sad by the pause between playing and eating, he had gone to the piano and had begun a piece by Mozart. It was the first time he had ever voluntarily gone to the piano. His sister left her picture book to dance to his music. (p. 37)
("Miss Lonelyhearts and the Clean Old Man," p. 24)	

His insertion of an extra detail for contrast made several scenes more dramatic and vital than they were in the original:

May, 1932	April, 1933
I consciously lost myself in an evening long past.	He forgot that his heart was a bomb to remember an incident of his childhood. (p. 37)
("Miss Lonelyhearts and the Clean Old Man," p. 24)	
I thought of children dancing.	As Miss Lonelyhearts stood at the bar, swaying slightly to the remembered music, he thought of children dancing.
("Miss Lonelyhearts and the Clean Old Man," p. 24)	
	(p. 37)

The elimination of a modifier strengthened the work in a few places:

February, 1932	April, 1933
He had played with this thing, but he never allowed it to come entirely alive.	He had played with this thing, but had never allowed it to come alive. (p. 20)
("Miss Lonelyhearts and the Lamb," p. 83)	

And the elimination of a subjunctive phrase served the same function by changing the figure from a simile to a stronger metaphor:

May, 1932	April, 1933
And on most days I received more than thirty letters, all of them alike, as though stamped from the dough of	And on most days he received more than thirty letters, all of them alike, stamped from the dough of suffering

suffering with a heart-shaped cookie   with a heart-shaped cookie knife.
knife.   (p. 2)
("Miss Lonelyhearts and the
Dead Pan," p. 13)

Occasionally the revision increased the sublety. In the novel there is
no forthright statement that the "clean old man" is really a homosexual, and the reader's curiosity remains delightfully unsatisfied; in
the original version, however, there was no question about it:

May, 1932	April, 1933
"Aw, come off," Gates said. "We're scientists. He's Havelock Ellis and I'm Krafft-Ebing. When did you first discover homosexualist tendencies in yourself?" "But I do like women, Mr. Ebing. When I was younger I . . ." ("Miss Lonelyhearts and the Clean Old Man," pp. 25–26)	"Aw, come off," Gates said. "We're scientists. He's Havelock Ellis and I'm Kraft-Ebing. When did you first discover homosexualistic tendencies in yourself?" "What do you mean, sir? I . . ." (p. 40)

And there are many examples of changes in single words in order to
create vividness and vitality: "bootlegger" for "ciderman," "bloody"
for "bloodstained," "punch in the mouth" for "blow in the mouth,"
and "fresh air" for "open air," for example.

Some of the revisions improved the finished work simply by being
more appropriate to the characterization. For example, in the revision
of the long letter from the poorly-educated Broad-Shoulders, "things"
replaced "articles" and "too many to write" replaced "too numerous to
mention." In another chapter Miss Lonelyhearts' own age was changed
from twenty to a much more likely twenty-six.[5] But other changes can
be attributed to no other reason than West's own preference. Three
times he changed the kind of alcohol, substituting brandy for cham-
pagne, beer for whiskey, and rye for whiskey in situations where it is
hard to see how it could have made any difference (pp. 21, 38, and
40). And occasionally a revision seems unquestionably detrimental.
One clear statement in the original became, when revised, ambiguous,
and in its revised state it also raises the question of why the feature
editor would be in charge of personnel:

[5] This change is in the *Contempo* chapter, and again there is room for suspicion
that the editors there may have changed it originally. Twenty seems far too young
in either the early or the revised version.

May, 1932	April, 1933
I would ask to be transferred to the sports department. ("Miss Lonelyhearts and the Clean Old Man," p. 24)	He would ask Shrike to be transferred to the sports department. (p. 38)

Another revision devitalized a scene by eliminating its shocking and hilarious repulsiveness and thereby reducing it to a rather ordinary incident:

October, 1932	April, 1933
He drew back when she reached for a kiss. She caught his head and put her tongue into his mouth. At first it ticked like a watch, then the tick softened and thickened into a heart throb. It beat louder and more rapidly each second until he thought that it was going to explode, and pulled away with a rude jerk. ("Miss Lonelyhearts on a Field Trip," p. 54)	He drew back when she reached for a kiss. She caught his head and kissed him on his mouth. At first it ticked like a watch, then the tick softened and thickened into a heart throb. It beat louder and more rapidly each second, until he thought that it was going to explode and pulled away with a rude jerk. (p. 66)

But these two examples are exceptions; there are very few instances in which the revised version is not manifestly better than the original.

Comparison of the early and late versions of these five chapters shows, then, not only that Nathanael West had a perceptive sense of literary structure and unity, but that he was as well a painstaking and astute reader and reviser of his own work. By experimenting with several methods of narration until he found the most appropriate one, by relocating various parts of the chapter so that the movement in each would be unrestricted and easily perceptible, by eliminating irrelevant themes and unifying those he retained, and by minutely reworking each individual sentence to condense and enliven it for the greatest possible impact, he showed himself to be a mature and conscious craftsman who knew the direction of his work of art and strove to make all its parts point in that direction.[6]

[6] I am deeply indebted to Prof. James B. Colvert of the University of Virginia, who made dozens of valuable suggestions while this study was in progress.

Some Notes on Miss L.

by Nathanael West

I can't do a review of *Miss Lonelyhearts*, but here, at random, are some of the things I thought when writing it:

As subtitle: "A novel in the form of a comic strip." The chapters to be squares in which many things happen through one action. The speeches contained in the conventional balloons. I abandoned this idea, but retained some of the comic strip technique: Each chapter instead of going forward in time, also goes backward, forward, up and down in space like a picture. Violent images are used to illustrate commonplace events. Violent acts are left almost bald.

* * *

Lyric novels can be written according to Poe's definition of a lyric poem. The short novel is a distinct form especially fitted for use in this country. France, Spain, Italy have a literature as well as the Scandinavian countries. For a hasty people we are too patient with the Bucks, Dreisers and Lewises. Thank God we are not all Scandinavians.

Forget the epic, the master work. In America fortunes do not accumulate, the soil does not grow, families have no history. Leave slow growth to the book reviewers, you only have time to explode. Remember William Carlos Williams' description of the pioneer women who shot their children against the wilderness like cannonballs. Do the same with your novels.

* * *

Psychology has nothing to do with reality nor should it be used as motivation. The novelist is no longer a psychologist. Psychology can become something much more important. The great body of case his-

"Some Notes on Miss L." by Nathanael West. From *Contempo* 3, no. 9 (May 15, 1933): 1–2. Reprinted by permission of S. J. Perelman and M. A. Abernethy.

tories can be used in the way the ancient writers used their myths. Freud is your Bulfinch; you can not learn from him.

*　　*　　*

With this last idea in mind, Miss Lonelyhearts became the portrait of a priest of our time who has a religious experience. His case is classical and is built on all the cases in James' *Varieties of Religious Experience* and Starbuck's *Psychology of Religion*. The psychology is theirs not mine. The imagery is mine. Chapt. I—maladjustment. Chapt. III—the need for taking symbols literally is described through a dream in which a symbol is actually fleshed. Chapt. IV—deadness and disorder; see Lives of Bunyan and Tolstoy. Chapt. VI—self-torture by conscious sinning: see life of any saint. And so on.

*　　*　　*

I was serious therefore I could not be obscene.
I was honest therefore I could not be sordid.
A novelist can afford to be everything but dull.

Symposium on *Miss Lonelyhearts* (1933)

Angel Flores: Miss Lonelyhearts in the Haunted Castle

Somebody mentioned Dostoevski and Cocteau as *Miss Lonely-hearts* progenitors. I had never seen such names coupled before. I re-read *Miss Lonelyhearts* and gradually the statement elucidated itself. In *Miss Lonelyhearts* do appear the hairshirts worn by Fyodor's heroes, and the air rings with antiChristian catapults, bloody guffaws and mystical quavers. The author of *Miss Lonelyhearts* has not tried to conceal his admiration for the Russian master. In fact the most exciting section in his earlier work, *The Dream Life of Balso Snell,* was significantly entitled *Journal of John Raskolnikov Gilson.* Dostoevski *is* a concomitant of *Miss Lonelyhearts*—but how about Cocteau? I did not see the point clearly perhaps because Cocteau has so many sides and the side my friend had in mind was not predominantly Cocteauan. What my friend really meant was that peculiar nightmarish quality, that pervasive uncanniness which hovers over the canvasses of Giorgio de Chirico and Salvador Dalí. In literature it existed, coarsely, in the terrorists of the XVIIIth century, in the Walpole-Reeve-Radcliffe trio, and, more particularly, in Lewis' *The Monk.* Later it entered the chapel of the Symbolists via Poe-Coleridge, and now reigns, stylized, in surrealisme. Mystery saturates the finest works of the day. Ribemont-Dessaignes Jouhandeau, René Char, Péret, Desnos, and to a lesser degree, Drieu la Rochelle and Henri Poulaille. And though at some distance from, say, *Confiteor*—one can sense it in such vastly different creations as *Der Steppenwolf* and *Geheimnis eines Menschen* . . .

Nathanael West's most remarkable performance has been to bring Fyodor's dark angels into the Haunted Castle. He did not recur to the drab realism which is so responsible for the stagnation in the works of the younger American writers—a realism which generally produces accurate reporting, easy-to-handle bulletins and timetables, and ALSO bad literature. Mr. West has given us anguish and terror and fantasy

"Miss Lonelyhearts in the Haunted Castle" by Angel Flores. From *Contempo* 3, no. 11 (July 25, 1933): 1–8. Reprinted by permission of M. A. Abernethy.

(Dostoevski-Ribemont-Dessaignes?) at the very crucial moment when the current vanguard taste insists on directing literature towards the casehistory, gravymashpotato tradition.

Josephine Herbst: Miss Lonelyhearts: *An Allegory*

Miss Lonelyhearts reads like a detective story. Its realism is not concerned with actuality but with the comprehension of a reality beyond reality. The furniture of the speakeasy, the upside-down quality of New York night and day life provide a background that only a fine movie camera could actually interpret. This crazy pattern fits the nightmare quality of the story of Miss Lonelyhearts, the newspaper columnist, who under a sentimental name acts high priest to the broken hearted whose letters begging advice pour into his sanctum. Actually *Miss Lonelyhearts*, the book, is a sort of allegory.

Miss Lonelyhearts floundering among the problems of humanity, stuck in the Slough of Despond of bankrupt emotionalism to the accompaniment of high powered motors, jazz music, weeping drunks and men out-of-work reflects much more than his own minute destiny. The entire jumble of modern society, bankrupt not only in cash but more tragically in emotion, is depicted here like a life sized engraving narrowed down to the head of a pin. Miss Lonelyhearts, stricken with the suffering of the underdog, seeks an answer. Flagellating himself with suffering, he in turn incurs suffering. His sadism breeds back upon himself and in bewilderment he turns to God, symbol of crucifixion and death. The pathological intensity of this seeking leads him to the desire to embrace humanity and that embrace pitches him to death. The ecstatic moment, realistically furnished, in which this occurs approaches the miracle of the old Mystery Plays.

It is significant that although all the scenes are not night scenes, in retrospect they appear to take place in semi-darkness, in that sort of twilight that occurs in dreams. The characters too are those of the dream, faces out of line, some distortion. Miss Lonelyhearts himself, in his dilemma, seeking a way out, is without distinct features. As he goes down, he seems to be someone wearing the huge nose of a clown who has been tightropewalking and has suddenly been discovered to have broken legs. He falls into the pit and even as he sinks the clown nose tortures us with a desire to laugh, the same kind of laughter that

"Miss Lonelyhearts: An Allegory" by Josephine Herbst. From *Contempo* 3, no. 11 (July 25, 1933): 1–8. Reprinted by permission of M. A. Abernethy.

hysterically crops up in a tragic moment. If the characters are not sharpened in an individualistic way it is because they much more nearly serve their purpose in this book as types. They are not Mrs. Jones or Miss Smith or Mr. Brown but the Desolates, the Heartaches, the Anxious of the world whose faces mask identical suffering more poignant than any individual difference.

Doomed by the society that roars around them to live ignominiously and alone in rabbit hutches, poking their heads out to wail to their father confessor, who, like them is lost, they are not puppets so much as they are representatives of a great Distress. Let anyone who thinks this implies a grotesqueness out of line with the strictest contemporary reality pick up any newspaper. Terror accompanied by the great wash of indifference is in every line. The Tom Mooneys rot in jail to an indifferent California, the Scottsboro boys wait in a destiny quite outside their comprehension or control. That Miss Lonelyhearts in his great need clutches at nothing better than God is symptomatic also. As he goes down in his bad luck the unsolved problems of Abandoned, Expectant and Despair must await some other deliverance.

William Carlos Williams: Sordid? Good God!

It's not only in the news section but among the feature sections also that newspapers show they have been published to conceal the news. West takes for his theme "The Miss Lonelyhearts of The New York *Post-Dispatch* (Are-you-in-trouble? Do-you-need-advice? Write-to-Miss-Lonelyhearts-and-she-will-help-you)" It is of course a man who runs the column.

Now this is a particularly sordid piece of business, this sort of feature, for it must be obvious that no serious advice can be given to despairing people who would patronize and even rely on such a newspaper office. The fact is that the newspaper by this means capitalizes misfortune to make sales, offering a pitiful moment's interest to the casual reader while it can do nothing but laugh at those who give it their trust.

Imagine a sensitive man running such a column, a man of imagination who realizes what he is doing and the plot is wound up. What cure? Why the only cure, so far as Nathanael West is concerned, the

"Sordid? Good God!" by William Carlos Williams. From *Contempo* 3, no. 11 (July 25, 1933): 1, 8. Reprinted by permission of M. A. Abernethy and of New Directions Publishing Corporation, agents for Mrs. William Carlos Williams.

only truth possible is "the truth"—along with the effects of the evil upon his protagonist. A particularly interesting short novel.

And for this, because the subject matter is sometimes rather stiff, a critic (after all, one must call them something) writing in one of our daily papers has branded the book itself as "sordid." Good God.

How much longer will it take, I wonder, for America to build up a cultural ice of sufficient thickness to bear a really first rate native author? It will happen sooner or later, it must, for we already have a few excellent craftsmen. But—to paraphrase the late Bert Williams— when? Apparently we still make the old and puerile error of finding a work, because its subject matter is unsmiling, serious or if the matter smiles then naturally the book must be light. And so, taking a sordid truth of city making and carrying the facts of the case through to an engrossing climax in brilliant fashion, the book cannot be anything else but sordid also!

If this is so, why then so is *Macbeth* sordid, so *Crime and Punishment,* so nearly the whole of Greek tragedy. And so's your old man. Blah. And that's what our standard American criticism amounts to: Roxy and the statues. Thin ice. We fall through it into mud up to our knees. And there is scarcely a place we can turn to for relief.

This isn't a perfect book, few first books are. But it is excellently conceived and written and it cannot be thrust aside in such slipshod fashion. There are many reasons why nearly everyone who would pick it up would enjoy it.

One thing which has perhaps aided in a careless dismissal of the book is West's insistence on extreme types in his narrative—really the people that newspapers do get letters from: the girl without a nose, the simpleminded child who was raped on the roof of a tenement, "Sick-of it all," "Broken hearted," "Desperate," "Disillusioned-with-tubercular-husband." But after all the use of such extreme types is preeminently the business of literature or we should never have had either Romeo and Juliet, Klytemnestra or Lazarus, whose function it has been to reveal and emphasize a point under observation from a logical intelligence of the facts. Even Betty the innocent if battered girl of the story must be carried down by this dreadful logic also. The fact that she does not become hard-boiled to the end being in itself an interesting sidelight on West's objective.

The letters-to-the-papers which West uses freely and at length must be authentic. I can't believe anything else. The unsuspected world they reveal is beyond ordinary thought. They are a terrific commentary on our daily lack of depth in thought of others. Should such lives as

these letters reveal never have been brought to light? Should such
people, like the worst of our war wounded, best be kept in hiding?

The characters in West's book, these people whom the newspapers
make a business of deceiving, are the direct incentive to his story, the
seriously injured of our civic life—although the cases occur everywhere,
even worse, perhaps, in the rural districts. The unbearable letters are
cited and then the moral bludgeoning which they entail is rapidly
sketched out before our eyes. Nothing more clearly upon the track of
classical precedent.

If our thought would evade such matters West doesn't. But it is
done with skill and virtuosity. It can skate. What is the figure that
Dante uses in the Inferno? It is Virgil. It is poetry (that is, good writing) which permits a man, but no ordinary man, to descend to those
regions for a purpose. It is the art of writing, in other words, which
permits the downward motion since when writing is well made it en-
livens and elevates the whole reader—without sweetening or benumb-
ing the sense—while he plunges toward catastrophe.

I'm not dragging in Dante to say West writes poetic prose. He
doesn't. But I am saying the book is written with skill, we are not
wiped around by sloppy narrative. The story, dreadful as it is, is presented tolerably to us, do what we may about the things presented. It's
no treatise, no cold dissection. It is the intelligence feelingly going
beside us to make it possible for us at the very least to look and to
understand.

Although Mary always grunted and upset her eyes, she would not
associate what she felt with the sexual act. When he forced this association, she became very angry. He had been convinced that her grunts
were genuine by the change that took place in her when he kissed her
heavily. Then her body gave off an odor that enriched the synthetic
flower scent she used behind her ears and in the hollows of her
neck. . . .

He found himself in the window of a pawnshop full of fur coats,
diamond rings, watches, shotguns, fishing tackle, mandolins. All these
things were the paraphernalia of suffering. . . .

Perhaps I can make you understand. Let's start from the beginning. A
man is hired to give advice to the readers of a newspaper. The job is a
circulation stunt and the whole staff considers it a joke. He welcomes the
job, for it might lead to a gossip column, and anyway he's tired of being
a leg man. He too considers the job a joke, but after several months of
it, the joke begins to escape him. He sees the majority of the letters
are profoundly humble pleas for moral and spiritual advice, that they

are inarticulate expressions of genuine suffering. He also discovers that
the correspondents take him seriously. For the first time in his life, he
is forced to examine the values by which he lives. This examination
shows him that he is the victim of the joke and not its perpetrator.

Then someone started a train of stories by suggesting that what they
all needed was a good rape.

"I knew a gal who was regular until she fell in with a group and went
literary. She began writing for the little magazines about how much
Beauty hurt her and dished the boy friend who set up pins in a bowling
alley. The guys on the block got sore and took her into the lots one
night. About eight of them. They ganged her proper."

Take it or leave it. It's impossible to quote effectively for anything
but a minor purpose but that's approximately what the prose is like.
It's plain American. What I should like to show is that West has a fine
feeling for language. And this is the point I shall stop on. Anyone
using American must have taste in order to be able to select from
among the teeming vulgarisms of our speech the personal and telling
vocabulary which he needs to put over his effects. West possesses this
taste.

Religious Experience in *Miss Lonelyhearts*

by Marcus Smith

The main critical issue concerning Miss Lonelyhearts is whether the title character and protagonist is a tragic saint or a psychotic fool. James Light, for example, champions the "saint" school by arguing that Miss Lonelyhearts is profoundly concerned with the search for "some spiritual reality to believe in and live by," a quest that ends in "tragic disillusionment":

> Miss Lonelyhearts, wishing to succor with love all the desperate of the universe and expecting to perform a miracle by which the cripple will be cured, runs rapturously toward Doyle. But there is no miracle. Instead Miss Lonelyhearts is shot by Doyle, destroyed, like Christ, by the panic and ignorance of whose whom he would save. Doyle, and in him suffering man, shatters the only solution to the intolerableness of man's pain, destroys the Christlike man who perceives that love and faith are the only answers to man's pain in a universe he cannot understand.[1]

The opposite view is represented by Arthur Cohen, who, in a *Commonweal* review of *The Complete Works of Nathanael West,* says that Miss Lonelyhearts' "Christ complex" is "precisely a complex, not a belief in specific documents of faith, not faith in any order of sacrament or scheme of salvation. It is a complex, a fixation of the mind." Miss Lonelyhearts, in Cohen's final evaluation, "misrepresents the world and is martyr to his misrepresentation." [2]

These contrary positions are not easily resolved. However, an extremely important clue is West's "Some Notes on Miss Lonelyhearts," published shortly after the novel. These "Notes," though brief and fragmented, tell us what West thought of his title character and name two key sources:

"Religious Experience in Miss Lonelyhearts" by Marcus Smith. From *Contemporary Literature* 9, no. 2 (Spring, 1968): 172–88. © 1968 by the Regents of the University of Wisconsin. Reprinted by permission of the publisher.

[1] *Nathanael West: An Interpretive Study* (Evanston, 1961), pp. 75, 86–87.

[2] "Nathanael West's Holy Fool," *Commonweal,* LXIV (June 15, 1956), 277.

Miss Lonelyhearts became the portrait of a priest of our time who has a religious experience. His case is classical and is built on all the cases in James' *Varieties of Religious Experience* and Starbuck's *Psychology of Religion.* The psychology is theirs not mine. The imagery is mine. Chapt. I—maladjustment. Chapter III—the need for taking symbols literally is described through a dream in which a symbol is actually fleshed. Chapter IV—deadness and disorder, see Lives of Bunyan and Tolstoy. Chapter VI—self-torture by conscious sinning: see life of any saint. And so on.[3]

This passage demonstrates, I think, that West did not view his protagonist as either a saint or a psychotic; instead, he suggests that these two categories, in the twentieth century at least, far from being exclusive of each other, are perhaps identical. On the one hand Miss Lonelyhearts is "a priest of our time," and at the same time he suffers from "maladjustment . . . deadness and disorder . . . self-torture by conscious sinning. . . ." West, therefore, did not consider the saintly madman (or the lunatic saint) an impossible figure. Furthermore, this view is supported and the role of West's protagonist clarified when we turn to West's acknowledged sources, William James and Edwin Diller Starbuck. For these philosophers, religious experience often contains irrational, subjective, and even psychotic elements, and the "psychology" of Miss Lonelyhearts is, indeed, theirs.[4]

James' *Varieties of Religious Experience* is by far the more important of the two sources, even though West indicates no priority. Starbuck's *Psychology of Religion* is the earlier work and is limited to a statistical study of religious conversion, mainly during adolescence, and chiefly among American Protestants. James' *Varieties,* originating as the Gifford Lectures on Natural Religion delivered at Edinburgh in 1901–1902, drew on Starbuck but ranged more widely and deeply

[3] *Contempo,* III, No. 9 (May 15, 1933), 1.
[4] Despite West's direct reference, critics have generally ignored the question of the influence of James and Starbuck. Light states that *"Miss Lonelyhearts* is indebted for its psychology to William James' *Varieties of Religious Experience"* (p. 95), but does not follow up the idea. Stanley Edgar Hyman in his monograph, *Nathanael West* (Minneapolis, 1962), p. 16, suggests that West's reference to James "may be Westian leg-pull." Victor Comerchero in *Nathanael West: The Ironic Prophet* (Syracuse, 1964), p. 81, merely quotes West's acknowledgment. The only study of this matter other than my own is Thomas Lorch's recent paper, "West's *Miss Lonelyhearts*: Skepticism Mitigated?" *Renascence,* XVIII (Winter 1966), 99–109. Lorch's discussion parallels my study in some respects, but his analysis remains quite general and he does not come to grips with the novel in detail. Furthermore, Lorch's conclusion that "West attaches more positive value to religious faith than has hitherto been allowed" (109) is quite different from mine.

into the philosophical as well as psychological significance of religious experience, before, during, and after conversion. Starbuck cannot, however, be ignored. Very often he and James describe the same or similar religious experience or psychological type. James' "Sick Soul," for example, corresponds roughly to Starbuck's period of "storm and stress," and the former's "Twice born soul" is analogous to the latter's "new life." Nevertheless, James is the more important of the two acknowledged sources and his "varieties" clarifies several of the characters in *Miss Lonelyhearts.*

West said the subject of the opening chapter of *Miss Lonelyhearts* was "maladjustment," and he is right if he means that Miss Lonelyhearts is unable to cope with either the large or the minute aspects of reality. The novel opens with his staring at Shrike's mocking prayer:

> Although the deadline was less than a quarter of an hour away, he was still working on his leader. He had gone as far as: "Life *is* worth while, for it is full of dreams and peace, gentleness and ecstasy, and faith that burns like a clear white flame on a grim dark altar." But he found it impossible to continue. The letters were no longer funny. He could not go on finding the same joke funny thirty times a day for months on end. And on most days he received more than thirty letters, all of them alike, stamped from the dough of suffering with a heart-shaped cookie knife. (p. 66)[5]

Miss Lonelyhearts' "maladjustment" coincides in several important ways with the religious variety James calls the Sick Soul. The Sick Soul is obsessed with the presence and force of evil, and is convinced that "the evil aspects of our life are of its very essence," and that "the world's meaning most comes home to us when we lay them [the evil aspects] most to heart" (p. 128).[6] Moreover, there are "shallower and profounder levels" of the Sick Soul phenomenon: "There are people for whom evil means only a mal-adjustment with *things,* a wrong correspondence of one's life with the environment" (p. 131). This Sick Soul can be cured "by modifying either the self or the things, or both at once" (p. 132). But, says James, "there are others for whom evil is no mere relation of the subject to particular outer things, but something more radical and general, a wrongness or vice in his essential nature, which no alteration of the environment, or any superficial rearrangement of the inner self, can cure, and which requires a supernatural remedy" (p. 132).

---

[5] All citations from *Miss Lonelyhearts* are from *The Complete Works of Nathanael West* (New York, 1957).

[6] I refer throughout to the Modern Library edition (New York, 1929).

Miss Lonelyhearts, considered as a Sick Soul, seems to partake of both the "shallower and profounder levels." The environmental conflict is implicitly present through most of the novel. But Miss Lonelyhearts in the early parts of the novel is primarily an example of the "profounder" Sick Soul, "which no alteration of the environment, or any superficial rearrangement of the inner self, can cure."

In his "Notes" West refers to Bunyan and Tolstoy, and it is in his lecture on the Sick Soul that James first uses the example of Tolstoy, whose melancholia he characterized as anhedonia; that is, the "passive loss of appetite for all life's values":

> In Tolstoy's case the sense that life had any meaning whatever was for a time wholly withdrawn. The result was a transformation in the whole expression of reality. When we come to study the phenomenon of conversion or religious regeneration, we shall see that a not infrequent consequence of the change operated in the subject is a transfiguration of the face of nature in his eyes. A new heaven seems to shine upon a new earth. In melancholiacs there is usually a similar change, only it is in the reverse direction. The world now looks remote, strange, sinister, uncanny. Its color is gone, its breath is cold. . . . (pp. 148–149)

Miss Lonelyhearts' view of the world is remarkably similar in the early part of the novel. In the second chapter, as he is walking to Delehanty's speakeasy, he crosses a small park:

> As far as he could discover, there were no signs of spring. The decay that covered the surface of the mottled ground was not the kind in which life generates. Last year, he remembered, May had failed to quicken these soiled fields. It had taken all the brutality of July to torture a few green spikes through the exhausted dirt. (p. 70)

The response here (echoing Eliot's *Waste Land* in its sterile imagery) marks Miss Lonelyhearts as a clear example of anhedonia. And James emphasizes that anhedonia is a subjective state of perception. In other words, the outer world is changed by the inner disturbance. Notice that West opens with, "*As far as he could discover,* there were no signs of spring," thereby signifying that within his objective omniscient frame, West is shifting to the morbid anhedonic point of view of Miss Lonelyhearts. On the next page, the same thing occurs: "*He searched the sky for a target.* But the gray sky looked as if it had been rubbed with a soiled eraser" (p. 71). Throughout the novel, West uses this biased point of view, in which the freedom of the omniscient method is combined with the subjective immediacy of his character's perceptions and responses.

James discusses the Sick Soul's quest for a "supernatural remedy." To the Sick Soul, "the happiness of Eden never comes again" (p. 153). Instead, when happiness does come to this type, it is "not the simple ignorance of ill, but something vastly more complex. . . . The process is one of redemption, not of mere reversion to natural health, and the sufferer, when saved, is saved by what seems to him a second birth, a deeper kind of conscious being than he could enjoy before" (p. 154).

The subject of "a second birth" and its relationship to *Miss Lonely-hearts* is important and I will return to it. What I want to discuss now is the relationship between Miss Lonelyhearts and Betty. In contrast to the Sick Soul, Healthy-Mindedness is what James calls the "once-born" consciousness, which develops "straight and natural, with no element of morbid compunction or crisis" (p. 81). The "once-born" personality is psychologically the reciprocal of the Sick Soul. Where the Sick Soul is morbid, filled with and overpowered by the sense of evil in the world, the Healthy-Minded person is cheerful and, in his optimistic outlook, unable even to comprehend evil. As in the case of the Sick Soul, James distinguishes between varieties of Healthy-Mindedness:

> In its involuntary variety, healthy-mindedness is a way of feeling happy about things immediately. In its systematical variety, it is an abstract way of conceiving things as good. . . . Systematic healthy-mindedness, conceiving good as the essential and universal aspect of being, deliberately excludes evil from its field of vision. . . . (pp. 86–87)

Turning to West's novel, we find at the heart of the relationship between Miss Lonelyhearts and Betty the conflict between his morbidity and her systematic optimism. Betty stands for order, simplicity, childish innocence. Miss Lonelyhearts "had once thought that if her world were larger, were *the* world, she might order it as finally as the objects on her dressing table" (p. 79). But he knows that "Her world was not the world and could never include the readers of his column. Her sureness was based on the power to limit experience arbitrarily" (p. 79). When Miss Lonelyhearts visits Betty in the fourth chapter, and after he has viciously grabbed her breast, Betty's reaction is only to ask, "Are you sick?" This infuriates Miss Lonelyhearts. He shouts at her: "What a kind bitch you are. As soon as anyone acts viciously, you say he's sick. Wife-torturers, rapers of small children, according to you they're all sick. No morality, only medicine" (p. 81).

James says antagonisms "may naturally arise" between the Sick Soul and the Healthy-Minded, because to "the morbid-minded way . . . healthy-mindedness pure and simple seems unspeakably blind and shallow. To the healthy-minded way . . . the way of the sick-soul seems unmanly and diseased" (p. 159). This is an extremely accurate description of the conflict between Betty and Miss Lonelyhearts in the first part of the novel. Thus, Betty insists that Miss Lonelyhearts is sick and in need of her care. He replies that she is limited and shallow, that she cannot clearly comprehend (as he can) the evil and suffering in the world. Later, when Miss Lonelyhearts has been in his room for two days in a state of collapse, Betty visits him ("I heard you were sick"), feeds him hot soup, and puts his room in order. She tries to convince him that he should quit the Miss Lonelyhearts job, or, in other words, arbitrarily divert his attention from disease and death and thereby become well. Betty's healthy-minded "weapon for self-protection against disturbance" offers itself to Miss Lonelyhearts. And his response is precisely that of the Jamesian Sick Soul: "You don't understand, Betty, I can't quit. And even if I were to quit, it wouldn't make any difference. I wouldn't be able to forget the letters, no matter what I did" (p. 106). The reason it would make no difference is, as James puts it, "morbid-mindedness ranges over a wider scale of experience" than healthy-mindedness (p. 160). Miss Lonelyhearts is psychologically unable to "limit experience arbitrarily," which is what Betty does to preserve her healthy-mindedness.

Furthermore, James, while describing both states as distorted, clearly sympathizes more with the Sick Soul than with the Healthy-Minded. One reason is the lack of tolerance in the latter: "If religious intolerance and hanging and burning could again become the order of the day . . . the healthy-minded would . . . show themselves the less indulgent party of the two" (pp. 159–160). But the main reason James rejects Healthy-Mindedness is that "the evil facts which it refuses positively to account for are a genuine portion of reality; and they may after all be the best key to life's significance, and possibly the only openers of our eyes to the deepest levels of truth" (p. 160).

A parallel distinction is implicit in *Miss Lonelyhearts*. While West obviously develops Miss Lonelyhearts as a Sick Soul, Betty's Healthy-Mindedness is not a viable alternative. She *does* offer Miss Lonelyhearts a way out, an escape from the ugly world of the letters into the bland world of an advertising agency, a wife, children, gingham curtains and a picket fence; but this alternative demands that Miss Lonelyhearts, like Betty, "limit experience arbitrarily." He cannot do so, and therefore he grows into an insane saintliness. This is, paradoxically, a psychological growth, a movement into a broader though destructive level of experience.

In the "process of redemption" Miss Lonelyhearts' Sick Soul goes through several stages, and in a number of ways conforms to the process of religious conversion as described by James and Starbuck. In the opening of the book, as we have seen, Miss Lonelyhearts, though sick, is a deliberate non-believer. Through the seventh chapter ("Miss Lonelyhearts on a field trip") we see him groping desperately for some tangible, secular escape from his morbid awareness of the world's evil. He tries liquor (Chapters Two and Five), semi-philosophic reading—*The Brothers Karamazov* (Chapter Three), Betty (Chapter Four), violence (Chapter Five), sex (Chapters Four, Six, and Seven)—and nothing helps much, for in Chapter Eight, after Mrs. Doyle has left him, "Miss Lonelyhearts became physically sick and was unable to leave his room" (p. 104). This is the first crisis, the first breakdown. But it also is the beginning of his redemption or rebirth, for when he awakes from his hallucinatory dream in which he makes "a gigantic cross," he is "weak, yet calm" (p. 105). The stability of his consciousness, though temporary, is the first stage in his development towards a second birth.

James has much to say about the redemptive process in his lecture, "The Divided Self, and the Process of its Unification." First, for the Sick Soul, "Peace cannot be reached by the simple addition of pluses and elimination of minuses from life" (p. 163). This describes Miss Lonelyhearts' efforts through the early chapters, his bouncing from one impulse to another in search of peace. That he does not find it is understandable, for as James remarks, "renunciation and despair . . . are our first step in the direction of the truth. There are two lives, the natural and the spiritual, and we must lose one before we can participate in the other" (p. 163). The early chapters of *Miss Lonelyhearts,* therefore, are a dialectic of loss. One by one Miss Lonelyhearts turns to possible *natural* outlets, the answers of this world, and one by one they prove inadequate. And in his frantic movement, Miss Lonelyhearts shows himself to be what James calls a "heterogeneous personality": "There are persons whose existence is little more than a series of zig-zags, as now one tendency and now another gets the upper hand" (p. 166). Bunyan (who is mentioned by West in his "Notes") is used by James as an example of a "Divided Self," a man religiously obsessed who could not, or would not, accept belief in Christ and was thrown into deepest despair by the struggle.

James considers the process of reunification a phenomenon not exclusively religious: "Religion is only one out of many ways of reaching unity" (p. 172). But whatever form it takes, it is "precisely the same

psychological . . . event—a firmness, stability, and equilibrium suc-
ceeding a period of storm and stress and inconsistency" (pp. 172–173).
Furthermore, "In the spiritual realm there are . . . two ways, one
gradual, the other sudden, in which inner unification may occur" (p.
180). Both Bunyan and Tolstoy are examples of "the gradual way,"
and West's specific reference to them makes sense, for Miss Lonelyhearts, too, is an instance of gradual unification, of wavering uncer-
tainty before the final completion of self. The "calm" Miss Lonelyhearts experiences in the eighth chapter is a momentary respite from
his sick morbidity, for in the following chapter he is still in bed: he
"realized that his present sickness was unimportant. It was merely a
trick by his body to relieve one more profound" (p. 111). And when
he goes with Betty to the Connecticut farm, he experiences merely a
relapse from the true process of unification going on inside him. The
farm and the pastoral setting cannot make him well, because he is the
more profound Sick Soul, and, as James notes, "no alteration of the
environment" can cure this type (p. 132). This explains Miss Lonelyhearts' reaction upon returning to the city: "When they reached the
Bronx slums, Miss Lonelyhearts knew that Betty had failed to cure
him and that he had been right when he had said that he could
never forget the letters. He felt better, knowing this, because he had
begun to think himself a faker and a fool" (p. 115).

Convinced now that environment is not the cause of his sickness,
Miss Lonelyhearts begins his quest for "humility." He finds that "the
farther he got below self-laughter," the easier humility is to practice.
This statement, coming at the beginning of the eleventh chapter, just
before Miss Lonelyhearts meets Doyle in Delehanty's, is an indication
of the progress he has made towards unification or "redemption."
Back in the second chapter, Miss Lonelyhearts had said that self-
laughter was a device he often used to protect himself: " 'Ah, humanity. . . .' But he was heavy with shadow and the joke went into
a dying fall. He tried to break its fall by laughing at himself" (p. 70).
Self-laughter is a defense against taking oneself too seriously. Therefore, Miss Lonelyhearts' "humility" is not humility at all but a kind of
egotistical obsession. The contradiction is apparent also in the statement that "Miss Lonelyhearts dodged Betty because she made him feel
ridiculous" (p. 121). That he should want to keep from feeling
ridiculous is the result of pride, not humility, for the truly humble
man is filled already with a sense of his own ridiculousness.

More importantly, however, Miss Lonelyhearts in Chapter Thirteen
has obviously been reborn:

He thought of how calm he was. His calm was so perfect that he could not destroy it even by being conscious of it. In three days he had gone very far. It grew dark in the room. He got out of bed, washed his teeth, urinated, then turned out the light and went to sleep. He fell asleep without even a sigh and slept the sleep of the wise and the innocent. Without dreaming, he was aware of fireflies and the slop of oceans. (p. 131)

Miss Lonelyhearts' equilibrium is difficult to explain in the context of the novel alone. Just previously, he had failed miserably in haranguing the Doyles that "Christ is love," and afterwards, "He felt like an empty bottle, shiny and sterile" (p. 129). Miss Lonelyhearts then finds, suddenly, the lasting spiritual unification for which he has searched throughout the novel. What is its cause? Part of the answer, I think, lies in James' discussion of the subconscious maturing process which produces sometimes startling results. James comments on the general phenomenon, using the example of the recollection of a familiar name:

> Usually you help the recall by working for it, by mentally running over the places, persons, and things with which the word was connected. But sometimes this effort fails: you feel then as if the harder you tried the less hope there would be, as though the name were *jammed,* and pressure in its direction only kept it all the more from rising. And then the opposite expedient often succeeds. Give up the effort entirely; think of something altogether different, and in half an hour the lost name comes sauntering into your mind, as Emerson says, as carelessly as if it had never been invited. Some hidden process was started in you by the effort, which went on after the effort ceased, and made the result come as if it came spontaneously. (p. 202)

Starbuck also describes this phenomenon: "The personal will must be given up. In many cases relief persistently refuses to come until the person ceases to resist, or to make an effort in the direction he desires to go" (pp. 113–114).[7] James gives Starbuck considerable credit for understanding this variety of conversion, known as "self-surrender," and his summary of Starbuck's exposition is excellent. Moreover, it very accurately describes what happens to Miss Lonelyhearts:

> Starbuck seems to put his finger on the root of the matter when he says that to exercise the personal will is still to live in the region where the imperfect self is the thing most emphasized. Where, on the contrary, the subconscious forces take the lead, it is more probably the better self

[7] I refer throughout to *The Psychology of Religion* (London, 1899).

in posse which directs the operation. Instead of being clumsily and vaguely aimed at from without, it is then itself the organizing centre. What then must the person do? "He must relax," says Dr. Starbuck—"that is, he must fall back on the larger Power that makes for righteousness, which has been welling up in his own being, and let it finish in its own way the work it has begun. . . . The act of yielding, in this point of view, is giving one's self over to the new life, making it the centre of a new personality, and living, from within, the truth of it which had before been viewed objectively." (p. 206)

Part of the reason for Miss Lonelyhearts' sudden "self-surrender" into conversion is that he has exhausted himself emotionally. His indifference is due to a draining of his energies. This is the reason he "had gone to bed again" (p. 131). It is also the reason he stands "quietly" in the center of the room when the drunken Shrike wants to fight. Miss Lonelyhearts is in the midst of what James calls the "state of temporary exhaustion [that] not infrequently forms part of the conversion crisis" (p. 208).

In the final chapters, Miss Lonelyhearts undergoes several of James' "varieties of experience," and, ironically, in the penultimate chapter, he is reborn into the realm of Healthy-Mindedness, where evil can not reign triumphant. In "Miss Lonelyhearts and the party dress," he deliberately refuses to be affected by Betty's sharpness; instead he maintains a forced gaiety and tranquility. Now it is Miss Lonelyhearts who smiles, who overrides the harsh facts with the force of his will. He begs Betty to marry him, promises to take the job at the advertising agency, and in general attempts to coerce reality into pleasant shapes. When Betty tells him she is pregnant, he simply proposes marriage and takes her home. "He did not feel guilty. He did not feel. The rock was a solidification of his feeling, his conscience, his sense of reality, his self-knowledge" (p. 138). "Solidification" here does not mean realization, but rather a state opposite his earlier storm-and-stress when feeling, conscience, reality, and self-knowledge were all a mad, whirling jumble. As James describes the process,

> So long as the egoistic worry of the sick soul guards the door, the expansive confidence of the soul of faith gains no presence. But let the former faint away, even but for a moment, and the latter can profit by the opportunity, and, having once acquired possession, may retain it. Carlyle's Teufelsdröckh passes from the everlasting No to the everlasting Yes through a "Centre of Indifference." (pp. 208–209)

The title of the last chapter, "Miss Lonelyhearts has a religious experience," alludes explicitly to James, and it is to this chapter and this experience that West points in his "Notes" when he describes Miss Lonelyhearts as "a priest of our time who has a religious experience." James devotes one of his later chapters to Mysticism, and what he has to say is directly related to the way West develops this final chapter. Essential to the mystic state, says James, is the penetration of the usual barriers separating the individual from the Absolute, whatever the Absolute may be for the given person: "In mystic states we both become one with the Absolute and we become aware of our oneness. This is the everlasting and triumphant mystical tradition, hardly altered by differences of clime or creed" (p. 410). This principle underlies Miss Lonelyhearts' experience in the final chapter:

> "Christ! Christ!" This shout echoed through the innermost cells of his body.
> He moved his head to a cooler spot on the pillow and the vein in his forehead became less swollen. He felt clean and fresh. His heart was a rose and in his skull another rose bloomed.
> The room was full of grace. A sweet, clean grace, not washed clean, but clean as the innersides of the inner petals of a newly forced rosebud.
> Delight was also in the room. It was like a gentle wind, and his nerves rippled under it like small blue flowers in a pasture.
> He was conscious of two rhythms that were slowly becoming one. When they became one, his identification with God was complete. His heart was the one heart, the heart of God. And his brain was likewise God's.
> God said, "Will you accept it, now?"
> And he replied, "I accept, I accept." (p. 139)

The mystic experience, according to James, is always distinguished by two features: *Ineffability* ("it defies expression . . . no adequate report of its contents can be given in words") and *Noetic quality* ("insight into depths of truth unplumbed by the discursive intellect"); in addition, two other features are "usually found": *Transiency* ("half an hour, or at most an hour or two, seems to be the limit") and *Passivity* ("the mystic feels as if his own will were in abeyance . . . as if he were grasped and held by a superior power" (pp. 371–372). These four characteristics apply accurately to Miss Lonelyhearts' mystic experience in the last chapter. The ineffability is seen in the imagistic description. The noetic quality is suggested (again through images) by "Christ is life and light" and "His heart was the one heart, the heart of God." Transiency is obvious: the entire description takes less than half a page. Likewise, Miss Lonelyhearts' will becomes the will of God, at least in Miss Lonelyhearts' mind: "He submitted drafts of his column to God and God approved them. God approved his every thought" (p. 139).

It is obvious, however, that Miss Lonelyhearts' mysticism in this final chapter is fatally mixed with Healthy-Mindedness, or at least one of the most striking features of Healthy-Mindedness, the belief in Mind-Cure. We have already noted how Miss Lonelyhearts seems to reverse roles with Betty in the penultimate chapter. There it is Betty who snaps, "What are you grinning at?" In the fourth chapter it was Miss Lonelyhearts who detested Betty's cheerfulness: "You have a smug smile; all you need is the pot belly" (p. 80). In the penultimate chapter, Miss Lonelyhearts has the "simplified mind" (p. 136); and it is he who believes (foolishly) that everything will turn out all right if only he thinks it will, if only he believes strongly enough that he can override the unpleasant, ugly facts of the situation. He says he will take the advertising agency job: "He was not deliberately lying. He was only trying to say what she wanted to hear" (p. 137). And when Betty announces her pregnancy, Miss Lonelyhearts "begged the party dress to marry him, saying all the things it expected to hear, all the things that went with strawberry sodas and farms in Connecticut" (p. 137). This is a new Miss Lonelyhearts, completely different from the morbid person who earlier declared "he could never forget the letters" (p. 115).

James says that "Mind-Cure" is characterized by "an intuitive belief in the all-saving power of healthy-minded attitudes as such, in the conquering efficacy of courage, hope, and trust" (p. 93). The results of this attitude, according to James, are that

> the blind have been made to see, the halt to walk; lifelong invalids have had their health restored. The moral fruits have been no less remarkable. The deliberate adoption of a healthy-minded attitude has proved possible to many who never supposed they had it in them: regeneration of character has gone on on an extensive scale; and cheerfulness has been restored to countless homes. (p. 93)

Thus Miss Lonelyhearts can ignore the facts of the situation (for one thing, he does not love Betty) and believe that by wishing it, everything will be set right. It is this belief in mind-over-matter, Mind-Cure, which gets him killed.

Peter Doyle arrives to defend or restore his wife's "honor." When Miss Lonelyhearts sees him "working his way up the stairs," he is certain that "God had sent him so that Miss Lonelyhearts could perform a miracle and be certain of his conversion" (p. 139). "He would

embrace the cripple and the cripple would be made whole again, even
as he, a spiritual cripple, had been made whole" (pp. 139–140). And
so, "He rushed down the stairs to meet Doyle with his arms spread for
the miracle" (p. 140). The miracle, ironically, is death, not the "life
and light" of Christ's crucifixion, and this is the final grotesque "religious experience" for Miss Lonelyhearts.

As for other varieties of religious experience, James distinguishes
between "shallower" and "more profound" mystical states. Miss
Lonelyhearts' orgiastic state in the final chapters is prefaced by some
of the simpler mystic states. "The simplest rudiment of mystical experience," says James, is "that deepened sense of the significance of
a maxim or formula which occasionally sweeps over one. . . . This
sense of deeper significance is not confined to rational propositions.
Single words, and conjunctions of words, effects of light on land and
sea, odors and musical sounds, all bring it when the mind is tuned
aright" (pp. 373–374). West, in the third chapter of *Miss Lonelyhearts*,
parallels James' "simplest rudiment of mystical experience." In this
chapter Miss Lonelyhearts reads a passage from *The Brothers Karamazov* and immediately starts reflecting on Christ and "how dead the
world is . . . a world of doorknobs" (p. 75). He recalls the religious
impulses of his childhood: "when he shouted the name of Christ, something secret and enormously powerful" stirred in him (p. 75).

Another type of "mystical" state, according to James, is the "consciousness produced by intoxicants and anaesthetics, especially by
alcohol. The sway of alcohol over mankind is unquestionably due to
its power to stimulate the mystical faculties of human nature, usually
crushed to earth by the cold facts and dry criticisms of the sober hour"
(p. 377). In the fifth chapter Miss Lonelyhearts goes to Delehanty's
speakeasy and "drank steadily" (p. 83). After a "train of stories . . .
suggesting that what they all needed was a good rape," Miss Lonelyhearts "stopped listening" to his friends and drifts away in his mind to
a recollection from his childhood:

> One winter evening, he had been waiting with his little sister for their
> father to come home from church. . . . he had gone to the piano and
> had begun a piece by Mozart. . . . His sister left her picture book to
> dance to his music. She had never danced before. She danced gravely
> and carefully, a simple dance yet formal. . . . As Miss Lonelyhearts stood
> at the bar, swaying slightly to the remembered music, he thought of
> children dancing. Square replacing oblong and being replaced by circle.
> Every child, everywhere; in the whole world there was not one child who
> was not gravely, sweetly dancing. (pp. 84–85)

As a unifying vision, an image of perfection (oblong: square: circle), Miss Lonelyhearts' dream qualifies as one of James' lower forms of mystical experience. But, of course, this is an inadequate form of mysticism (as was the type mentioned before) and it ends with abrupt violence when Miss Lonelyhearts turns from the bar and gets punched in the mouth. The effect of the punch (besides a loosened tooth) is to bring him back to the world of reality: "His anger swung in large drunken circles. What in Christ's name was the Christ business? And children gravely dancing?" (p. 85).[8]

Finally, at the highest level, comes the direct mystical union with the Absolute, and earlier I quoted the passage in which Miss Lonelyhearts experiences it. Just before this union with God, Miss Lonelyhearts

> fastened his eyes on the Christ that hung on the wall opposite his bed. As he stared at it, it became a bright fly, spinning with quick grace on a background of blood velvet sprinkled with tiny nerve stars.
>
> Everything else in the room was dead—chairs, table, pencils, clothes, books. He thought of this black world of things as a fish. And he was right, for it suddenly rose to the bright bait on the wall. It rose with a splash of music and he saw its shining silver belly. (pp. 138–139)

West's description here is similar to James' discussion of *The Spiritual Exercises* of Saint Ignatius Loyola. Ignatius, says James, tells "the disciple to expel sensations by a graduated series of efforts to imagine holy scenes. The acme of this kind of discipline would be a semi hallucinatory mono ideism—an imaginary figure of Christ, for example, coming fully to occupy the mind. Sensorial images of this sort, whether literal or symbolic, play an enormous part in mysticism" (pp. 397–398). West very carefully follows this pattern. First, Miss Lonelyhearts expels extraneous, distracting sensations by fastening his eyes on the crucifix. Immediately he sees a series of shifting images and symbols which are clearly "semi-hallucinatory" and which culminate

---

[8] It is also in this chapter that a specific echo of James occurs in the remark by one of Miss Lonelyhearts' friends that "he's a leper licker. Shrike says he wants to lick lepers. Barkeep, a leper for the gent" (p. 89). This is almost certainly based on James' discussion of saintliness and the extremes to which holy people have gone in their love: "The nursing of the sick is a function to which the religious seem strongly drawn. . . . But in the annals of this sort of charity we find fantastic excesses of devotion recorded which are only explicable by the frenzy of self-immolation simultaneously aroused. Francis of Assisi kisses his lepers . . . St. John of God, and others are said to have cleansed the sores and ulcers of their patients with their respective tongues" (p. 279).

in the rising fish image. This step is followed immediately by his realization that "Christ is life and light."

The fish symbol, from ancient times a symbol for Christ, is most striking and corresponds remarkably to Starbuck's description of the sensation of conversion. Most of Starbuck's subjects were not able to describe their moment of conversion, but Starbuck notes that "two persons illustrated graphically the process by drawing lines. In both, conversion was pictured by rapidly ascending curves" (p. 190). The image of the fish rising in Miss Lonelyhearts' consciousness so nearly conforms to Starbuck's "rapidly ascending curves" that West may very well have been thinking of the earlier psychological work at this point, despite West's claim that the imagery of *Miss Lonelyhearts* was his own.

I earlier raised the problem of whether Miss Lonelyhearts is sick or saintly. I think he is, indeed, "sick," but this opinion, too, needs to be qualified by reference to James. In his opening lecture, "Religion and Neurology," James clearly states that he is not concerned with "individuals for whom religion exists . . . as a dull habit," but instead he is interested in those "religious geniuses" for whom religion is "an acute fever":

> such religious geniuses have often shown symptoms of nervous instability. Even more perhaps than other kinds of genius, religious leaders have been subject to abnormal psychical visitations. Invariably they have been creatures of exalted emotional sensibility. Often they have led a discordant inner life, and had melancholy during a part of their career. They have known no measure, been liable to obsessions and fixed ideas; and frequently they have fallen into trances, heard voices, seen visions, and presented all sorts of peculiarities which are ordinarily classed as pathological. Often, moreover, these pathological features in their career have helped to give them their religious authority and influence. (p. 8)

West's development of Miss Lonelyhearts seems to parallel James' idea that exceptional religious experience is intrinsically combined with "peculiarities which are ordinarily classed as pathological." As much is implied in West's comment that while Miss Lonelyhearts is suffering from "maladjustment" he is also "a priest of our time who has a religious experience." Thus, at times we justifiably sympathize with Miss Lonelyhearts—in the scenes between him and Shrike, for instance. On the other hand, Miss Lonelyhearts is quixotic: despite his "great understanding heart," he can be detached, and sometimes even viciously contributes to the pain which so greatly distresses him. He hardly struggles at all when he commits adultery with Fay Doyle, so anxious is he for sexual release. And in one of the novel's perfectly ironic scenes he practically tears an old man's arm off thinking all the time that "he was twisting the arm of all the sick and miserable, broken and betrayed, inarticulate and impotent. He was twisting the arm of Desperate, Broken-hearted, Sick-of-it-all, Disillusioned-with-tubercular-husband" (p. 88). Miss Lonelyhearts here is reacting to his own sickness, frustration, and misery, his own sense of betrayal, his own inarticulateness and impotency, and West clearly intends us to see his violent actions as ironic contradictions.

Thus the question of Miss Lonelyhearts is not easily answered. But whether Miss Lonelyhearts is *ultimately* a religious man is a question that James would consider irrelevant. For James (and West as well, I think) the final validity of religious belief and behavior is beyond understanding. James' pragmatic approach to the subject led him to disavow the possibility (and even the desirability) of understanding the supernatural origins and bases of religious experience. It was James' purpose to describe, from a scientific rather than a metaphysical point of view, that area of human experience known as "religious." Similarly, in *Miss Lonelyhearts,* West's concern with religious belief is limited to this world. Miss Lonelyhearts is driven to Christ because of the situation in this world and the need for answers here, not in the hereafter; he is not concerned with immortality, supernatural reality, or problems of theology. He is obsessed by the sterility of this "world of doorknobs," and his problem is partly whether belief in Christ is "too steep a price to pay" to bring this dead world to life. This is a pragmatic consideration, and it is precisely this point of view which James uses to determine the value of religious belief.

Briefly, James' argument is that "God is real since he produces real effects" (p. 507). By this James means that the belief in God causes men to have a variety of experiences (classified as "religious"), and experience is reality, at least the only reality open to understanding. Furthermore, religious experience is to be judged by its effects. Thus confession can be valid because "for him who confesses, shams are over and realities have begun; he has exteriorized his rottenness" (p. 452). Prayer, also, can justify itself apart from any supernatural order: "in certain environments prayer may contribute to recovery, and should be encouraged as a therapeutic measure" (p. 453). Sacrifice, on the other hand, when it consists of "burnt offerings and the blood of he-goats," is nothing but vain oblations" (p. 452).[9]

[9] James' remarks about sacrifice perfectly describe the "vain oblations" in the third chapter, "Miss Lonelyhearts and the lamb."

When we apply this pragmatic Jamesian standard to *Miss Lonely-hearts,* we get a negative answer to the question of the value of religious experience. Miss Lonelyhearts' religious experience does not help him to cope with reality, even though he thinks it does. To the contrary, it leads him to his destruction, and by implication his death means additional suffering for Doyle, Betty, and the child within her. Light, therefore, is wrong when he argues that the message of *Miss Lonelyhearts* is that "the love and faith of Christ are the only solutions in which man can rest." In terms of the novel itself and from the standpoint of James' criteria, Miss Lonelyhearts' religious quest is a false one.

The Waste Land of Nathanael West

by Edmond L. Volpe

Nathanael West's *Miss Lonelyhearts* has too long been denied recognition as one of the great short novels in American Literature. West's masterful use of poetic imagery in the novel form is incisive, brilliant; his story is powerful, its emotional impact overwhelming, its significance profound. Technically, the novel is marred, to some extent, by a loss of artistic control in the final chapters, but despite this flaw, the book deserves a niche in the history of American Literature, not only on the basis of literary merit, but also because it is the answer of the 1930's to the great poem of the 1920's—T. S. Eliot's *The Waste Land*. I do not know whether West intended his novel as a reply to Eliot. The similarities in theme and imagery seem too obvious to be accidental. West's intentions, at any rate, are of little significance: his novel is an answer to the optimism implicit in Eliot's vision of man and society. Though Eliot's poem is a somber and depressing view of modern man and his culture, it is a view brightened by hope. Eliot's optimism is particularly obvious when his vision is contrasted with West's.

*　　*　　*

The unnamed protagonist of *The Waste Land* (West's protagonist, too, is unnamed, though in an earlier version published in part in *Contact*, he is named) is throughout the novel on a pilgrimage. He moves through the waste land of his soul and of his society seeking salvation. The land he inhabits is a world without values, a mechanical world reflecting the aridity in the soul of modern man. There were times in human history, the poem informs us, when man was vibrant with life: he had ideals, moral values and responded to basic natural forces. Modern man, however, is sexually impotent, morally sterile,

"The Waste Land of Nathanael West" by Edmond L. Volpe. From *Renascence* 13 (Winter, 1961): 69–77, 112. Reprinted by permission of the author and the publisher.

culturally stagnant. He is a mechanical man, physically alive, spiritually dead. The land is arid because man's soul is arid. Since the Waste Land is man-made, it is within man's power to regenerate his dead world. In the final section of the poem, the protagonist discovers the means of salvation—religious belief. Though he is not yet ready to achieve his salvation, the method is available to him. Eliot's Waste Land is not the product of forces beyond human control. There is supreme order in the universe. Man, individually, need only submit to God, the source of that order. By submitting, man can bring order into his own soul and thereby into his world.

As depressing as Eliot's vision may be, therefore, it is far from pessimistic. West's vision, in contrast, is terrifyingly pessimistic. His waste land, which is symbolized in part by the park between the newspaper office and the speakeasy, in many ways resembles Eliot's: "As far as he could discover, there were no signs of spring. The decay that covered the surface of the mottled ground was not the kind in which life generates. Last year, he remembered, May had failed to quicken these soiled fields. It had taken all the brutality of July to torture a few green spikes through the exhausted dirt."

It, too, is a spiritually barren world in which an adding machine ritual replaces older religions, a culturally sterile land in which the people "have dissipated their radical energy in an orgy of stone breaking." The inhabitants of West's waste land, as I shall presently show, are similar to the inhabitants of Eliot's. The major difference in the two visions is in the cause of the cultural and moral aridity. To West, the human being appears a misfit in an undirected universe: "Man has a tropism for order. . . . The physical world has a tropism for disorder, entropy." Man cannot impose order on the universe. With his dreams—his religions, his philosophies, his art, his science—he has tried to establish order, but history and time have proved his efforts futile. Evil, the manifestation of the world's disorder in human existence, has always flourished. The heroic ages Eliot recalls in his poem are for West simply periods in which men's illusions and dreams were more powerful, and therefore more effective in disguising the realities. And the realities in human existence are the entropy of the physical world and man's supreme need for order. But every "order has within it the germ of destruction. All order is doomed, yet the battle is worth while."

The battle is the alternative to suicide, but how does man battle? "Men have always fought their misery with dreams." West's tragic vision of human life is the same vision Eugene O'Neil dramatized in *The Iceman Cometh,* probably the most despairing play of our time. Both writers see man's ideals and ideas as nothing but pipe dreams. These empty dreams, as man's only defense against the brutality of reality, are essential if he is to go on living.

I make much of West's despair because it is the fact that eluded me when I first read *Miss Lonelyhearts.* The columnist's plight is so pathetic, his desire to succor his fellow sufferers so attractive, his Christ dream so appealing that he remains a sympathetic character to the end of the novel. Miss Lonelyhearts in the final chapters, however, is a madman; he has severed all contact with reality. The theme of the novel demands that the reader experience pity, not sympathy, for Miss Lonelyhearts in his madness; but West, in his final chapters, does not exert sufficient artistic control over his story and his own feelings (I suspect) to withdraw his reader to an observer's position. Let me document these general statements by analyzing the novel.

Like Eliot's protagonist, the hero of *Miss Lonelyhearts* is given the opportunity to view the waste land in which he lives. What both protagonists see, as I indicated previously, is a world without values. There is one major difference: Miss Lonelyhearts' world has no values, not because man has thrown them over, substituting superficial values for good ones, but because the human being has reached a time in his history when he can no longer delude himself. None of his philosophies or dreams has ameliorated or accounted for the presence of evil, for the pain, the suffering, the misery of human existence. In the three letters that open the novel, the writers are victims, completely innocent victims, of forces beyond their control. They in no way deserve the suffering they are undergoing. Sick-of-it-all is being tortured by her husband, whose blind faith in Catholicism has made him the destructive agent of a concept. Religion, which should be providing Sick-of-it-all comfort in her distress and a reason for living, is destroying her. Desperate is born without a nose. She pleads with Miss Lonelyhearts to tell her why she deserves such a fate. Harold S. begs advice about his deaf and dumb thirteen year old sister who has been raped by a stranger and is now to suffer the social humiliation of an unwed mother. Each letter describes a natural or human force of evil that crushes man in a vise of anguish. For these sufferers the flame of their agony is reality. Their protective illusions have burned away. But reality cannot be endured without dreams, and in desperation the anguished victims write to Miss Lonelyhearts. The unknown writer of the newspaper column becomes their only hope of salvation; in his column they seek "The Word."

Miss Lonelyhearts' waste land, therefore, is more than a reflection of man's personal and cultural degeneration; it is a land in which evil and human suffering stalk in their naked horror. No sensitive viewer of this land can observe the anguish and retain his sanity. The inhabitants of the waste land are, from necessity, breathing dead men. The death mask is their alternative to facing the horrors of life. The chief spokesman of these inhabitants is Shrike, named for the butcher bird that impales its prey on a thorn or twig while tearing it apart with its sharp hooked beak. Shrike is a "dead pan . . . his features huddled together in a dead, gray triangle," one of the crowd flowing over London bridge in Eliot's "Unreal City" passage. Shrike, like all human beings, must have some defense against reality. One of the nasty products of "this unbelieving age," he lives by impaling the dreams of others and ripping them apart: he makes a joke of everything. He and his fellow newspapermen had "believed in literature, had believed in Beauty and in personal expression as an absolute end. When they lost this belief, they lost everything." Their dream destroyed, they became "machines for making jokes. . . . They, no matter what the motivating force, death, love, or God, made jokes." Shrike's wife, Mary (Belladonna, the Lady of the Rocks), is incapable of giving herself sexually, and her husband, in love with her, comforts himself with cruel jokes and with the sterile sex of the "Miss Farkises of this world" who "had long legs, thick ankles, big hands, a powerful body, a slender neck and a childish face made tiny by a man's haircut."

Miss Lonelyhearts, too, had been a joke machine until the column he had begun as a joke forced him "to examine the values by which he lives. This examination shows him that he is the victim of the joke and not its perpetrator." He is the victim because the people he had planned to laugh at reveal to him the horrors of life; their agonized pleas penetrate to his heart. He can no longer ignore the reality of human existence. Like Melville's Captain Ahab, West's Miss Lonelyhearts concludes that there is no such thing as justice in the universe; human evil is merely an eruption of universal evil. The two characters experience the same awful insight. Their subsequent madness takes different forms because they are a century apart in the history of man. There is no fight in the twentieth century columnist, no need for vengeance. Captain Ahab had something to hate, something to struggle against. He could defy the gods, hate the injustice of the universe, reject the cruelty of man. Miss Lonelyhearts has no opponent: "He searched the sky for a target. But the gray sky looked as if it had been rubbed with a soiled eraser. It held no angels, flaming crosses, olive-bearing doves, wheels within wheels. Only a newspaper struggled in the air like a kite with a broken spine."

There is nothing to blame, no God to hold responsible. By becoming Miss Lonelyhearts, the newspaperman had drawn back his protective curtain of illusion. The sight of naked horror the letters bring to his view destroys his mental and emotional stability, placing him on the very edge of madness. When he looks up to the sky for a target and can find none, Miss Lonelyhearts has reached that moment of complete despair that the French existentialist writers a few years later were to term *Nauseé*, or The Absurd. Miss Lonelyhearts' creator, however, was no existentialist. He could not move out of his despair; he could only joke about man's attempt to curtain reality, write a satire on the Christ dream—the salvation of Eliot's Waste Land.

On the edge of madness when the novel opens, Miss Lonelyhearts struggles to save himself. Two methods of salvation are available to him. He can try to ignore the sight he has seen and forget it in some personal escape dream; or he can face the horror and try to bring solace to the sufferers by providing them with some dream to replace those they have lost. His sensitivity and sympathetic nature force him to take this latter method. He realizes that he shall never be able to forget the pain he has witnessed. The columnist is a reader of the *Brothers Karamazov*; Father Zossima's advice, to love man even in his sin, excites him. He envisions himself teaching the whole world to love. Man would no longer be cruel. "The kingdom of Heaven would arrive. He would sit on the right hand of the Lamb." Also, Miss Lonelyhearts is the son of a minister. "As a boy in his father's church, he had discovered that something stirred in him when he shouted the name of Christ, something secret and enormously powerful. He had played with this thing, but had never allowed it to come alive." Miss Lonelyhearts, therefore, has a readily available emotional recourse in his moment of need. "He knew now what this thing was— hysteria, a snake whose scales are tiny mirrors in which the dead world takes on a semblance of life. And how dead the world is . . . a world of doorknobs. He wondered if hysteria were really too steep a price to pay for bringing it to life."

The Christ dream for Miss Lonelyhearts, in other words, is a form of madness; it can cut him off from reality, making the dead world seem alive. As a product of his age, however, Miss Lonelyhearts cannot rationally accept Christ, and religion is meaningless to him. In a dream sequence, his desire to help his fellow men and his inability to accept religion as a means of salvation are symbolized. He first sees himself as a magician on a stage, performing tricks with doorknobs (dreams). He is successful with his tricks, but when he tries to lead his audience in prayer the only prayer that comes to mind is a cynical parody that Shrike, who echoed Miss Lonelyhearts' rational self, had taught him. In his first dream the columnist desires to lead his audience out of the waste land, but he cannot because he lacks conviction. In the second dream scene the ritual of animal sacrifice (reminiscent of the primitive rites referred to by Eliot) is no recourse for modern man. Miss Lonely-hearts and the two college companions with whom he had been arguing about the existence of God are unable to perform the sacrificial ceremony. Out of pity Miss Lonelyhearts goes back to kill with a stone (throughout the novel a symbol of despair) the wounded lamb, the traditional symbol of Christ.

Miss Lonelyhearts knows, therefore, that if he gives himself over to the Christ dream he will be cutting himself off from reality. But what else can he offer Sick-of-it-all and Broken Hearted, whose own dreams have evaporated in the hellish flames of reality? He is their last hope, and he cannot ignore them. He must help his fellow men, suffer for them, become the living Christ. Christ is his natural inevitable haven, though he realizes it is an empty dream. Christ, as Shrike declares, is the Miss Lonelyhearts of Miss Lonelyhearts—the ultimate, vacuous hope of the desperate. The columnist also knows that "Even if he were to have a genuine religious experience, it would be personal and so meaningless, except to a psychologist." The Christ dream, Nathanael West is saying, can perhaps provide personal escape, but it is not the salvation of the waste land; it is not, as in Eliot's poetry, the means of personal and thereby universal salvation.

The intensity of Miss Lonelyhearts' need drives him toward the Christ dream; the knowledge that Christ is no more than a dream drives him away. Torn in two, he moves toward the abyss of madness. He hesitates before he plunges over the brink, wondering if hysteria—madness—is too steep a price to pay. Eventually he realizes it is not, but first he tries a series of personal escapes, all of which fail because he cannot forget the cries of anguish and choke off his need to help his fellow men.

He goes to visit Betty, his fiancée. The visit is a failure; Betty and her ordered life are intolerable to him because her "sureness was based on the power to limit experience arbitrarily. Moreover, his confusion was significant, while her order was not." Betty, whom Chance has spared, lives within a tiny bright circle of personal peace by ignoring the shadows that surround her. She refuses to acknowledge the existence of evil. " 'No morality, only medicine,' " says Miss Lonelyhearts, describing her attitude. Human cruelty is not a manifestation of evil for Betty; it is sickness. And sickness can be cured. There is nothing fundamentally wrong with the universe; there are only minor aberrations.

Betty provides no escape, so at Delehanty's the columnist tries alcohol. Temporarily it is successful; he slips into a genial haze that makes him immune to the jokes of his fellow drinkers. He remembers an incident from his childhood: he is playing the piano and his sister responding happily to the music. He envisions children everywhere dancing in ordered natural motions of happiness. The thought of children revives the Christ dream. Reality shatters the moment of peace. He is punched in the mouth by a man whom he accidentally bumps as he turns from the bar. Miss Lonelyhearts becomes angry with himself for giving in to the dream. And at the end of the drunken evening he meets an aged homosexual. Alcohol has not blunted his sensitivity to suffering and he reacts as he had done many years before when he accidentally stepped on a small frog. "Its spilled guts had filled him with pity, but when its suffering had become real to his senses, his pity had turned to rage and he had beaten it frantically until it was dead." And so he beats up the pervert, trying symbolically to erase the suffering he can do nothing to lessen.

Alcohol fails to relieve his agony and so does his next attempt at escape—sex. For Mary Shrike, sex can be nothing but an unending game. Though Miss Lonelyhearts has played the sterile game with her before, in desperation—but without desire—he plays the game once more. To some extent he succeeds in shutting out the rest of the world. "He feels an icy fatness around his heart." The thought that the nightclub they go to is simply a more expensive type of dream than those offered by advertisements to develop biceps or busts merely irritates him. "For the time being, dreams left him cold." But he cannot escape. His sexual advances are countered with dreams. Mary talks of her parents, of her mother's death, of her father. "Parents are also part of the business of dreams. . . . People like Mary were unable to do without such tales." For a moment before Miss Lonelyhearts leaves Mary, he almost loses himself in awakened desire. The game ends; Mary rushes into her apartment where Shrike awaits her.

The next day at his desk, Miss Lonelyhearts envisions a desert of rust and body dirt in which Desperate and Broken Hearted are forming the letters of Miss Lonelyhearts' name with white-washed clam shells, products of the sea, the symbol of rebirth, regeneration. He reads Fay Doyle's letter, tries to "discover a moral reason" for not responding to her invitation, concluding that if "he could only believe in Christ, then adultery would be a sin, then everything would be simple and the letters extremely easy to answer." He cannot. He dismisses his Christ dream and tries sex once again. The meeting with Mrs. Doyle is reminiscent of the fertility rites Eliot makes allusions to in his poem, in which water serves as the regenerating medium. Mrs. Doyle is the sea, Miss Lonelyhearts the carcass thrown into the water. "She made sea sounds. . . . Her call to him to hurry was a sea-moan, and when he lay beside her, she heaved, tidal, moon-driven. Some fifteen minutes later, he crawled out of bed like an exhausted swimmer leaving the surf."

The ritual fails; sex is no escape for him or for Mrs. Doyle. Sitting on his lap, she tells him her life story and the "life out of which she spoke was even heavier than her body. It was as if a gigantic, living Miss Lonelyhearts letter in the shape of a paper weight had been placed in his brain."

This failure pushes Miss Lonelyhearts closer to madness. He becomes physically ill and spends two days in bed. He recognizes, however, that his "present sickness was unimportant. It was merely a trick of his body to relieve one more profound." His tension has increased. He pictures himself before the show window of a pawn shop, and with the forsaken possessions of the desperate he builds a phallus, a heart, a diamond, a circle, triangle, square, swastika, the symbols of men's dreams that have failed. "But nothing proved definitive, and he began to make a gigantic cross." He moves the cross to the ocean and adds to it with the refuse of the sea.

Betty comes to offer him an escape to simple country life, away from the city where so much human misery is concentrated. Another visitor, Shrike, arrives to describe with cynical eloquence and dismiss with cynical eloquence all the personal means of salvation available to Miss Lonelyhearts: the simple country life and absorption in the basic rhythm of nature, the South Sea Islands, the pursuit of pleasure, art, suicide, and drugs. None of these escapes can serve the sick man. As he listens, he thinks of "how Shrike had accelerated his sickness by teaching him to handle his one escape, Christ, with a thick glove of words."

Miss Lonelyhearts is ready now to give in to the hysteria. Betty, however, insists that he try the country life. He accompanies her to the Connecticut farm and for a few days he does know a measure of tranquility, even sexual satisfaction. He has entered, momentarily, Betty's world of limited experience. As soon, however, as they reach the Bronx slums on their return drive, "Miss Lonelyhearts knew that Betty had failed to cure him and that he had been right when he had said that he could never forget the letters."

Salvation that does nothing to ameliorate the general suffering is not for him. The Christ dream with its promise of universal love and universal salvation must be his dream. To placate his rational self, Miss Lonelyhearts, prodded "by his conscience . . . began to generalize. . . . Although dreams were once powerful, they have been made puerile by the movies, radio, and newspapers. Among many betrayals, this one is the worst. The thing that made his share in it particularly bad was that he was capable of dreaming the Christ dream. He felt he had failed at it, not so much because of Shrike's jokes or his own self-doubt, but because of his lack of humility."

The sick man is close to his release from reality. Humility and brotherly love flood his heart. Momentarily successful in his endeavor to surround everyone with love when Fay Doyle's crippled husband appeals to him for help in Delehanty's, Miss Lonelyhearts attempts to extend his success and unite the husband and wife with love. His failure is comically tragic. During the supper, he envelops them with his beatific smile, ignoring Fay's hand on his thigh beneath the table. He searches for a message that will convey his dream, that will bring the Kingdom of Heaven to the estranged couple. His words embarrass the Doyles "By avoiding God, he had failed to tap the force in his heart and had merely written a column for his paper." A second more hysterical message makes him feel like "an empty bottle, shiny and sterile." His own salvation, the Christ dream, cannot be communicated. His dream is menaced by Fay who thrusts herself at him and makes him feel like "an empty bottle that is being slowly filled with warm, dirty water." Miss Lonelyhearts staves off this intrusion of reality by beating Fay Doyle until she releases her hold on him.

The columnist's growing spiritual isolation is reflected in his physical separation from the world. He jams his telephone and locks himself in his cell-like room. His only nourishment is crackers and water. ("When they ask for bread don't give them crackers as does the Church," Shrike had joked.) At the end of the three days of symbolic entombment, Miss Lonelyhearts arises. His suffering is over; he has become the rock. West's use here of the symbol of despair, the rock, to symbolize his protagonist's withdrawal from reality makes clear his attitude toward the Christ dream. (The symbol may also be a satirical reference to the effectiveness of the Church in aiding suffering mankind.) And the sea, the regenerative symbol, is now, ironically, applied to the world from which Miss Lonelyhearts has withdrawn.

The rock is twice tested. Shrike dashes into the sick man's room, "but fell back, as a wave that dashes against an ancient rock, smooth with experience, falls back." Shrike's jokes, which had become increasingly cynical as Miss Lonelyhearts moved deeper into his dream, reached their climax with the Miss Lonelyhearts game, a cruel, inhuman, gigantic joke with the columnist as its butt. Miss Lonelyhearts is impregnable. "What goes on in the sea is of no interest to the rock." The second trial is more severe. Betty is pregnant and announces she wants an abortion. Her fiancé argues against it, asks her to marry him, promises to give up his column, leave the newspaper, and accept her world of limited experience. He tells her everything she wants to hear, lying blithely, feeling no remorse. "He did not feel guilty. He did not feel. The rock was a solidification of his feeling, his conscience, his sense of reality, his self-knowledge." Though Miss Lonelyhearts' withdrawal from life is complete, his absorption in the Christ dream has one final phase. The next day the columnist becomes feverish; he hears the voice of God and, submitting, he achieves the peace which passeth understanding. (Eliot: "Then spoke the thunder . . . *Datta*") His "identification with God was complete. His heart was the one heart, the heart of God." West's next sentence, as a prelude to Miss Lonelyhearts' final act, is brutally ironic: "And his brain was likewise God's."

When Miss Lonelyhearts hears Peter Doyle toiling up the stairs, he rushes from his room with outspread arms to perform a miracle. He will make the crippled man whole as he, a spiritual cripple, has been made whole. The Christ dream has become a delusion: Miss Lonelyhearts is mad. Mistaking Doyle's cry of warning as an anguished plea for help, he runs to succor the cripple and all the other sufferers of the world. Frightened, Doyle turns to escape. Miss Lonelyhearts grabs him. When Betty enters, Doyle tries to get rid of the pistol wrapped in newspaper. The gun goes off; the columnist falls. The shooting lacks the dignity of a deliberate act; it is accidental: order cannot be imposed on a world that has a tropism for disorder.

*   *   *

Nathanael West keeps his point of view intact throughout his novel except in one scene: that in which Miss Lonelyhearts slips away from

Shrike's party. The single, sudden shift away from the consciousness of Miss Lonelyhearts may have been designed to withdraw the reader's sympathy from the protagonist. The artistic maneuver fails; the inhumanity of Shrike's joke is far more repulsive than Miss Lonelyhearts' delusion. When the reader is returned in the next scene to the hero's consciousness, he is more inclined to sympathy than before, a feeling, I imagine, that West himself had and could not control. The artistry of most of the novel is so deliberate that one is forced to conclude that these final chapters are confused because West was strongly attracted to, even if he could not believe in it, the Christ dream. Despite the confusion, West does make clear his intentions and his theme.

Miss Lonelyhearts is a brilliant, profound expression of despair, able, a quarter century later, to evoke the feeling and mood of its period better than any other novel, including *The Sun Also Rises*. Reading the novel is a painful emotional experience, not unlike that produced by reading *The Waste Land*. But in Eliot's Waste Land regeneration is possible; in West's there is no hope of salvation.

"Anywhere Out of This World":
Baudelaire and Nathanael West

by Marc L. Ratner

In recent years the work of Nathanael West has received something more than passing attention, and this in spite of the fact that he was neither a prolific nor a particularly influential writer. Essentially it was his view of American life and the "human condition" that has given his work a greater scope and importance than much American literature of the last three decades. His writing was distinctly different from most of the "proletarian" literature of the thirties; he attacked the false dreams symptomatic of the American *malaise* rather than the sterotyped "big bosses" and deputy sheriffs who figured so prominently in fiction of the time. The European tone of his writing, that is, his rejection of reform and his belief in the absurdity of existence, has its source in the French Symbolists and particularly Baudelaire. Critics have claimed that psychological studies provided West with his ideas, but he clearly limits the novelist's use of these sources in a short essay, "Some Notes on *Miss Lonelyhearts*":

> Psychology has nothing to do with reality nor should it be used as motivation. The novelist is no longer a psychologist. Psychology can become something much more important. The great body of case histories can be used in the way the ancient writers used their myths. Freud is your Bulfinch; you can not learn from him.[1]

It is true that he used the technique of leaving his material "almost bald," as a psychological case history, yet this stylistic economy is one of the prevalent features of the prose poetry of the French Symbolists

"'Anywhere Out of This World': Baudelaire and Nathanael West" by Marc L. Ratner. From *American Literature* 31 (January, 1960): 456–63. © 1960 by the Duke University Press. Reprinted by permission of the author and the publisher.

[1] *Contempo*, III, 2 (May 15, 1933).

also. West does comment on the way he develops his chapters by saying that *Miss Lonelyhearts* was a "novel in the form of a comic strip." He wrote, "Each chapter instead of going forward in time, also goes backward, forward, up and down in space like a picture." [2] West indeed regarded the novel as a series of concentrated incidents which revealed the psychological states of his main character, Miss Lonelyhearts: each cartoon panel presented a different mental condition. The prose poems of the French Symbolists are generally designed to create the same concentrated effect that West is concerned with here. West's style is a study in economy and directness, one which makes use of poetic imagery to attain the desired degree of concentration, and West's thoughts are identical to those of the Symbolists on this subject. "Lyric novels," he wrote, "can be written according to Poe's definition of a lyric poem." [3] His fiction generally shows the influence of the Symbolists because of its terse epigrammatic style, poetic imagery, and satiric content.

In one of his literary essays, Edmund Wilson says of Nathanael West, "He had been influenced by those post-war Frenchmen, who had specialized with a certain preciosity, in the delirious and diabolic fantasy that descended from Rimbaud and Lautréamont." [4] Though Mr. Wilson is no more specific than this, the influence of the French Symbolists is clearly evident in West's four novels: *The Dream Life of Balso Snell* (1931), *Miss Lonelyhearts* (1933), *A Cool Million* (1934), and *The Day of the Locust* (1939).[5] But more specifically, it is my contention that the pivotal experience of *Miss Lonelyhearts*—the discussion in chapter seven of the alternatives of escape—had its source in Baudelaire's prose poem "Anywhere Out of This World (N'Importe Où Hors Du Monde)," [6] and that a comparison of the two selections sheds light on the theme and format of West's novel.

That Baudelaire's poem was known to West is indicated by his use of the title in his first novel, *The Dream Life of Balso Snell*. In that book, the poet-hero while wandering through the ruins of Troy finds the Wooden Horse which symbolizes the world of art. He decides to enter it, but before doing so, he recites a prayer, "O Beer! O Meyer-

[2] *Ibid.,* p. 1.

[3] *Ibid.*

[4] Edmund Wilson, "The Boys in the Back Room," *Classics and Commercials* (New York, 1950), p. 52.

[5] *The Complete Works of Nathanael West* (New York, 1957). All references to West's novels will be to this edition of his works, cited in the text.

[6] Charles Baudelaire, *Petits Poèmes en Prose (XLVIII), Oeuvres Completes* (Paris, 1899), IV, 140–141.

beer! O Bach! O Offenbach! Stand me now as ever in good stead"
(p. 3). The incantation recalls the last line of Joyce's *Portrait of the
Artist as a Young Man,* and reflects West's ridicule of the artistic world.
Balso enters the horse's "posterior opening of the alimentary canal"
(p. 4) and shuts himself within the lonely world of his imagination.
To buoy his spirits he creates a song about the roundness of his new
cosmos, the womblike world in which he now finds himself. As a
possible title for the song, Balso thinks of *"Anywhere Out of This
World, or a Voyage Through the Hole in the Mundane Millstone."*
Despite the involved symbols and allusions in *Balso Snell,* the hero
remains a passive creature throughout most of the novel. It is only
in *Miss Lonelyhearts,* West's next novel, that his hero emerges into
the world and that "preoccupation with the self" gives way "to an
identification with society." [7]

In "Anywhere Out of This World," Baudelaire holds a conversation
with his soul. He regards life as a hospital in which the patients long
to change their beds; the question is "where?" The poet presents a
variety of escapes beginning with the inert, indolent existence of the
reptile. He offers the soul a life in Lisbon where, "Il doit y faire chaud,
et tu t'y regaillardirais comme un lézard." [8] Next, he offers a life of
involvement in human affairs in Holland, a land of tranquillity, where
one can see not only forests of ships' masts but also the craft moored
at the doors of houses. The poet then suggests escape to the East
Indies, to Batavia where the intellect of Europe and the beauty of
the tropical East are fused. To all of these possibilities the soul remains mute, responding with neither sound nor sign. Finally, the
poet suggests the lands which are like death, Tornio in Finland, the
utmost limits of the Baltic, the North Pole, where variety is impossible.
Here is "la monotonie, cette moitiè du néant." [9] At last the soul
explodes and wisely cries, "N'importe où! pourvu que ce soit hors de
ce monde!" [10]

Baudelaire's poem demonstrates that the prose poetry of the Symbolists was concerned less with narrative than with the presentation
of a succession of psychological states conveyed by symbols or allusive
language. West employs the same technique throughout much of

---

[7] Alan Ross, "The Dead Center: An Introduction to Nathanael West," *The
Complete Works of Nathanael West,* p. xiii.
[8] Baudelaire, *Oeuvres Completes,* IV, 140. ["It must be warm there, and you could
laze in the sun as contentedly as a lizard." —Ed.]
[9] *Ibid.,* p. 141. ["that monotony, which is the counterpart of nothingness." —Ed.]
[10] *Ibid.* [Anywhere! So long as it is out of this world!" —Ed.]

Miss Lonelyhearts with each chapter reflecting the psychological states of Miss Lonelyhearts, a male advice-to-the-lovelorn editor with a Christ complex. This technique appears at its best in chapter seven, "Miss Lonelyhearts in the Dismal Swamp." More important, one can see the influence of the content of Baudelaire's poem as well.

After a series of violent episodes in the earlier chapters, Miss Lonelyhearts is visited in his room by Betty, his girl-friend. She suggests that they go away for a few days in the country. But Betty is suddenly driven out of the room by the shouts of the drunken Shrike, a pitiless feature editor. Seizing upon her last remarks about life and love on the farm, Shrike sarcastically envisions the flight from the city and all that it entails, the rhythm of work, the "sexual step of a dance-drunk Indian" treading "the seed down into the female earth" (p. 107). Miss Lonelyhearts, like Baudelaire's soul, does not answer; he only considers how in the past Shrike had accelerated his sickness by "teaching him to handle his one escape, Christ, with a thick glove of words" (p. 107). Shrike continues with the South Sea Island escape in which the secret of happiness lies in a totally unreal Polynesian world created by Hollywood. Miss Lonelyhearts, again not answering, feigns sleep, but Shrike undeterred continues with the next possibility, Hedonism. He recommends that intellectual and physical pleasures be combined in sexual intercourse beneath the paintings of Matisse and Picasso. One departs stoically at the end of such a life, without complaint, playing the game. Again Miss Lonelyhearts is silent. Next Shrike offers aesthetic escape through art and the intellectual life, the spiritual rewards of which are superior to any of the previous offers. Without elaboration he mentions suicide and drugs briefly. Thus far his suggestions to Miss Lonelyhearts' soul have paralleled those of Baudelaire's prose poem in working through various forms of escape from human misery. But in the poem it is here that the poet's soul cries out, "Anywhere! Anywhere! Out of this world!" By way of parallel, Shrike offers the final escape, the one which Miss Lonelyhearts ultimately chooses, the escape "out of this world" to Christ.[11]

At this juncture Shrike dictates a letter to Christ, the "Miss Lonelyhearts of Miss Lonelyhearts." It is the climax of the novel since after

[11] Malcolm Cowley (*Exiles Return*, New York, 1951, pp. 237–240) saw this particular passage as a reflection of the artist's desire to escape from the conforming mass of the business civilization. But Miss Lonelyhearts' escape, though partially motivated by the rejection of the false dreams of American civilization, has a more profound basis than this, a point which becomes clearer through a comparison with Baudelaire's poem.

this chapter Miss Lonelyhearts begins his climb to an ultimate mystic union with God. The "Leopard of Discontent, the Lion of Discouragement" lie within and without his city. Like Dante, whose images West uses in Shrike's letter, Miss Lonelyhearts seeks faith in the dark wood and begins his way to union with God (pp. 107–110).

In the first seven chapters of the novel, Miss Lonelyhearts tries to rid himself of his Christ complex, first by withdrawal, then by violence and finally by immersing himself in a sexual sea. None of these purgatives are satisfactory, especially the last, which leaves him physically ill. In an article in *Contempo* magazine, West discussed the general technique which he employed in *Miss Lonelyhearts,* that of presenting a series of psychological states:

> Miss Lonelyhearts became the portrait of a priest of our time who has a religious experience. His case is classical and is built on all the cases in James' *Varieties of Religious Experience* and Starbuck's *Psychology of Religion.* The psychology is theirs not mine. . . . Chapt. I—maladjustment, Chapt. III—the need for taking symbols literally through a dream in which a symbol is actually fleshed. Chapt. IV—deadness and disorder; see Lives of Bunyan and Tolstoy. Chapt. VI—self-torture by conscious sinning; see life of any saint. And so on.[12]

West's "holy fool" [13] has reached the dark night of his soul; he is disgusted with a world much like Baudelaire's, a hospital where he and the sick persons who write to him want to change their beds. "Miss Lonelyhearts in the Dismal Swamp," then, becomes the central chapter of the novel. It begins with a dream in which Miss Lonelyhearts, entering the chaos of a pawnshop, attempts to set all in order by forming the odd assortment of objects into some sort of form, a phallus, a diamond, various geometric figures, and finally, a cross. This last form assumes such gigantic proportions that Miss Lonelyhearts has to move everything to a beach, where he tries unsuccessfully to include all the debris there into the giant cross (pp. 104–105). He awakens from his sleep to discover Betty, his girl-friend, who has

---

[12] *Contempo,* III, 2.

[13] Arthur Cohen, "Nathanael West's 'Holy Fool,'" *Commonweal,* XLIV, 276–278 (June 15, 1956). Mr. Cohen writes: "In *Miss Lonelyhearts* West attempted to make a statement of what happens to 'the holy fool' in the modern world. He is not treated as a mad saint and revered for his sanctity and the divinity of his madness. . . . He misapprehends the world because he is not capable, as modern man is generally not capable, of maintaining any distance from the world, any perspective or quiet before it."

the "ability to put her universe in order," [14] but whose order is false because it "excludes not only suffering but also the spiritual needs of man." [15] Though her simple back-to-nature formula is not successful in helping Miss Lonelyhearts solve his problem, she does provide an opening for Shrike, who bursts in at that moment. He first indicts the solution Betty has offered and then violently ridicules other forms of escape from existence. In the original manuscript, Miss Lonelyhearts himself mocked these forms of escape,[16] but in the final version Shrike, his verbally violent alter ego, provides the solutions. Where Shrike's violence is verbal, Miss Lonelyhearts' has been physical. In attempting to sacrifice a lamb to God, he succeeds only in making a disgusting job of it. He fights in a bar, tries to seduce Shrike's wife, and sadistically tortures an old man in a men's room. It is Shrike who at this point voices Miss Lonelyhearts' own materialistic views and his disgust with them. And it is Shrike whose sarcastic description of Miss Lonelyhearts' alternatives of escape is exactly what the mentally torn hero would say to himself.

In an article, *"Miss Lonelyhearts*: The Imagery of Nightmare," James F. Light has noted several similarities between Miss Lonelyhearts and Shrike, especially in the attempts of the former to reject the spiritual within him and to find the answer in the feature editor's materialism.[17] This certainly is true in the early chapters of the novel. Yet, as Mr. Light also points out, Miss Lonelyhearts proceeds to reject the materialism of Shrike. Despite the violence of his former acts, Miss Lonelyhearts, after Shrike's monologue, undergoes a change. Though Shrike derisively attacks God as an escape, Miss Lonelyhearts realizes that the "anywhere out of this world" exists in Christ through love. He is overwhelmed by a desire to help the "broken hands and torn mouths" (p. 115), and by a feeling of humility which grows within him like a rock. His sexual experience with Betty, unlike those with Mrs. Shrike and Mrs. Doyle, one of his unhappy correspondents, is a fulfilment, a creative act. When Mrs. Doyle had tried to excite him, he had felt "like an empty bottle that is being slowly filled with warm, dirty water" (p. 130). Shrike's remarks no longer reach Miss Lonelyhearts, who withstands his at-

[14] James F. Light, *"Miss Lonelyhearts*: The Imagery of Nightmare," *American Quarterly*, VIII, 319 (Winter, 1956).
[15] *Ibid.*
[16] *Ibid.*, p. 321.
[17] *Ibid.*

tacks when he reappears to belabor him with more letters of misery. He possesses "the utmost serenity. . . . What goes on in the sea is of no interest to the rock" (p. 134). After Miss Lonelyhearts leaves, Shrike gives an account of a "ladder of love" on which the love-lorn editor is mounting to Christ. Though Shrike is sarcastic, it is nonetheless an accurate account of Miss Lonelyhearts' "way." In the next to last chapter, after he has persuaded Betty to have their child, his one truly creative act, Miss Lonelyhearts is prepared for the final stage of his climb out of the pit of night—communion with Christ. His room is "full of grace"; he sees the figure of life and light before him; his heart and brain unfold like the White Rose of Dante's *Paradiso*; his religious experience is that of the mystic in complete union with God. "He was conscious of the two rhythms that were slowly becoming one. When they became one, his identification with God was complete" (p. 139). Spiritually "out of this world," he runs down the stairs to embrace and heal the cripple, Doyle, who is seeking revenge for being cuckolded. But Miss Lonelyhearts is killed by the accidental explosion of Doyle's gun. The absurdity and irony of his death has a point in relation to Baudelaire's prose poem. Miss Lonelyhearts, like the poet's soul, rejects the escapes through false dreams which the world offers, and at the end of the novel rushes literally "out of this world."

One might argue that Miss Lonelyhearts rushes down the stairs to perform the miracle which would make him "certain of his conversion" (p. 139), and that he is not desirous of death. This point can be further corroborated by Miss Lonelyhearts' plan for his new life and future conduct. However, despite his plans for the future, he has become impossible for the world just as the world has become impossible for him. Two critics makes the point that Doyle is directly responsible for Miss Lonelyhearts' death. E. G. Schwartz calls him "the murderer Doyle." V. S. Pritchett says Doyle "shoots him in a fit of jealousy." [18] But these statements are not accurate, since West explicitly indicates that Doyle cannot carry out the act. The cripple tries to escape Miss Lonelyhearts and to get rid of the package. In doing so, he takes his hand from the inside of the package, the gun explodes by itself and Miss Lonelyhearts falls.[19] His death by the accidental

[18] V. S. Pritchett, *"Miss Lonelyhearts,"* New Statesman, LIV, 791 (Dec. 7, 1957); E. G. Schwartz, "The Novels of Nathanael West," *Accent*, XVII, 256 (Autumn, 1957).

[19] Joran Mjöberg in an article, "Nathanael West: en ironisk patetiker," *Bonniers Litterara Magazin*, XXV, 133–137 (1956), criticizes the way West ended his novel.

explosion of a *mechanical* thing is the final irony. Miss Lonelyhearts' death is more than an ironic twist, for given West's view of the sordidness and futility of human existence, the most logical ending for Miss Lonelyhearts *is* to be destroyed by a cold, mechanical thing. At the end of Miss Lonelyhearts' "mystic way" lies failure because of the pointlessness of loving in a world that is dead to love. He leaves enwrapped in his final dream, the only one possible for him.

In discussing West's novels, Mr. Schwartz stated that the novelist's pessimism was deeper in *Miss Lonelyhearts* because dreams cannot work in the modern world even as escapes, and that there is no escape from the sceptical rationalist.[20] Mr. Light also comments on the inadequacy of modern dreams; but he talks of Miss Lonelyhearts' becoming "dead to the world," his detachment from the sea of life.[21] The novel has often been regarded as an example of West's despair. But though the Christian "dream" had lost its reality for some of West's critics, and for West himself, it had a real meaning for Miss Lonelyhearts. As Mr. Hollis puts it: "Miss Lonelyhearts was what West dared not be; Shrike was what he dreaded to become." [22]

In Baudelaire's poem all dreams are false, meaningless. One must leave the world because no dream can sustain the soul for any length of time. The soul in Baudelaire's poem is never deluded by suggested escapes, *sagement* [wisely] it cries out, "to leave the world." For Miss Lonelyhearts the one dream which has any meaning is the way of Christ. That West's view is closer to Baudelaire's can be seen in the senseless, pathetic death of Miss Lonelyhearts.

He points out that *Miss Lonelyhearts* has three alternatives: disintegration, middle-class life with Betty, or a life in Christ; but Mjöberg complains that a man with West's control should not have allowed his book to end in such an uncontrolled manner, that is, through the use of *deus ex machina*. My contention, of course, is that West never lost control of his subject.

[20] *Accent*, XVII, 257.

[21] *American Quarterly*, VIII, 319.

[22] C. C. Hollis, "Nathanael West and Surrealist Violence," *Fresco*, VII, 5–13 (1957).

Introduction to *Mademoiselle Côeur-Brisé* (*Miss Lonelyhearts*)

by Philippe Soupault

Those who admire New York, even those who love it, know that it is a cruel city. There is nothing easier than to be gay in New York, except to be sad. One need only move to another quarter, or let an hour go by, or turn a corner, or glimpse the interior of an apartment, or meet a man, either to burst into laughter or feel overcome by anguish. In the eyes of a black sitting on the sidewalk on 59th Street opposite the Hotel Plaza I have seen all the misery in the world, and at Times Square a few hours later I have run into a dazzling incarnation of youth, a blond girl, smiling, triumphant, radiant, "as beautiful as the day."

Of all the men I have known Nathanael West knew his way about New York and how to talk to New Yorkers best. He also knew how to describe their practices, whether admitted or not, their regrets and their remorse, the pains they take to find a moment of joy, or to avoid ruin. He was a man whose eye passed so quickly over people and things that he managed to see what other observers, more deliberate in their scrutiny, fail to see. His very appearance—he was tall and thin, fine drawn, his hair brown with red glints, with brilliant dark eyes, a nose like a knife-blade, and, at the time I knew him, sported a little mustache that had the air of a mask over his thick red lips—gave the distinct impression that this man with the ready smile, sometimes a little melancholy, was an authentic New Yorker. He never tried to shock his listeners, but what he said was always mildly startling. A casual remark of his would haunt you through the streets and avenues of New York. This quiet way of expressing

himself, of putting you on your guard, always whetted your desire
to know more. But you would not insist, because he did not insist.
I knew that he had been a journalist after leaving college, and that
he had got into journalism by the side door. When I knew him he
was no longer very young, for he had already observed a great deal,
as if driven by a passion to see all. (He never tired of observing things.)
At that time he was engaged in running a hotel. This occupation (for
it is not quite a craft, nor yet a science, but rather an art) allowed
him to make a penetrating study of the public or private lives of those
transients, men and women both, who turn up at the desk of high-rise
hotels as if summoned before the bar of justice. For a novelist this
calling is among the most fruitful one can find for being free to write
what one wants to write. In any case Nathanael West could read
the destiny of his guests in their hands and foresee how they might
behave during their stay, particularly those who, as soon as they enter
a hotel lobby, seem under compulsion to take on the air of malefactors
pursued by the police, as if they have committed some offense or perhaps even a crime.

How and why did Nathanael West choose the heroes of his novels?
I venture to say that no writer worthy of the name chooses his heroes,
but that in some curious way they choose their novelist. All that a
novelist can do is to prefer one to another. Thus Nathanael West preferred New York and New Yorkers, those most typical of New York.

With a skill we must admire, because it does not depend on trickery
or the kind of illusion used by prestidigitators who falsely pretend to
the high title of magicians, the author of *Miss Lonelyhearts* has taken
apart the mechanism of one of one of the most infernal machines of
American journalism, that which sets off the most explosions and
produces perhaps the largest number of casualties. In the popular
press of the United States, a woman, generally of a certain age, conducts a column in which she offers counsels of wisdom to desperately
unhappy people. She writes prudent, respectable, vague answers to
letters sent in by her readers, male or female, letters generally as stupid
as they are hopeless, as cruel as they are mad. This unscrupulous
woman (for who would dare to judge a case after having read a single
foolish letter, full of anguish? Who would pretend to be able to offer
useful advice without knowing all the circumstances?), this woman
receives mail in such quantities as to make the sports editor pale with
envy. Her correspondents write so fully and with such lack of reserve
that it borders on exhibitionism. Men and women alike make public
confession (for they all expect that their letters will be published) and

display their shameful actions along with their sufferings. It has been estimated by students of circulation trends that such correspondents are the most faithful readers of the newspapers. For this reason they are treated with consideration, and the woman who answers their letters is often the best paid contributor on the staff. To save money some editors have entrusted the lovelorn column to a young man who assumes the role at a lower salary. "Miss Lonelyhearts" is a young man who started out in the newspaper business as a reporter and ends up in this morass. He has in effect become the old lady without fear and without reproach.

Nathanael West knew Miss Lonelyhearts well. Like her (or like him) he has received similar letters, letters profoundly disturbing because they are so numerous and so pressing, and because they come day after day without fail, a constantly repeated groan of agony, an interminable lament like an air raid siren that means death for some people, a cry in the desert. No one wants to hear that woeful chant of pain that rises from all parts of New York, as in other great cities. There are some who will not hear it, who pretend to be deaf. But the voices of pain, misery and suffering cannot be stilled.

Nathanael West is probably (a polite way of speaking) the one writer of his generation—the generation of Hemingway, Faulkner and Caldwell—who has most willingly accepted the knowledge that he is an American. He has not sought excuses, he has not relied on the prestige of descriptive skill, or local color, or the mirage of the unconscious. He is as direct as an arrow and as sharp as a scalpel. While his contemporaries, the writers of the lost generation, never hesitated to say too much, West could never bring himself to say enough. From his conversation or his books one had the impression that he gave forth only what he thought to be not so much the essential as the most significant. He was as concise as others (numerous among American writers) are prolix. I am sure that he too could have disclosed secrets that everyone knows, or given tongue to characters released by alcohol or enflamed by madness. But for West there was not only *the sound and the fury,* there was also that deep laughter that rises from the entrails and transforms a smile into a grimace.

Thus West has suggested to the men of his generation—and it is this, in my view, that gives his work its value—that they should refuse to be taken in by anything. Now in the United States, more than in any other country, one is always in danger of entrapment by what appears on the surface to be a happy civilization. There is a sort of obligation to be happy. It is, by the way, so stated in the Declaration of Independence. Whoever is unhappy is suspect. Almost all American novelists, even if they do not admit it, adhere to the principle that we are born to be happy. Nathanael West has flatly rejected this principle.

As a witness and a seer, Nathanael West is missed and will be missed even more in the new epoch that is about to begin in New York. Never more than during this last year have I regretted the loss of the creator of *Miss Lonelyhearts*. The automobile accident in which he died is one of those news items that make one distrustful of fate. Nathanael West did not complete his work. What he did leave us remains among the most significant testimonials one can ask for in literature.

The Black Hole of Calcoolidge

by Jay Martin

> Oatsville is in Vermont. The Vermont of nutmegs, blue-berries and maple sugar. The Vermont of potbelly stoves, and cracker barrels. Cal Coolidge's Vermont.
> Joe Williams is one of Oatsville's nicest boys, blue-eyed, fair-haired, with a back as straight and strong as one of his mother's hickory chairs.
> A hero out of Horatio Alger.
> Only fools laugh at Horatio Alger, and his poor boys who make good. The wiser man who thinks twice about that sterling author will realize that Alger is to America what Homer was to the Greeks.
>
> —*A Cool Million: A Screen Story.*
> Treatment by Nathanael West and
> Boris Ingster (1940)

"I finally got started on my new novel and have been doing nothing else since," West wrote to George Brounoff in October, 1933. "I like it, and I think it'll be alright. You know I never wrote steadily before, taking a month to do five pages in the past, and find it hard to keep going. However, I'm doing five hours a day steadily now and expect to be on Harcourt's Spring list." He did move rapidly and by late autumn, still conceiving of this novel as a satire on the American Dream of Success, he was well along. Surely, never before in America had success seemed so unlikely or hope for success so vain. It was no accident that Josephson's *The Robber Barons,* Lewis Corey's *The Decline of American Capitalism,* Edward Dahlberg's *Those Who Perish,* and West's novel should all appear in the same year, when the extent to which Roosevelt's legislative program ran counter to *laissez faire* doctrine was becoming clear. Earlier American writers like Twain and Dreiser had rejected the Gospel of Success; but now this gospel was opposed very widely in America.

But West's anatomy of success had deeply personal as well as widely social roots. He could trace the effects of the gospel of success in his own life. Humbert Wolfe, among other theorists of satire, has suggested that "the satirist must have love in his heart for all that is threatened by the objects of his satire." [1] There is no doubt that the idea of success was highly charged for West. As a violent inversion of the American dream, *A Cool Million* provided West a means whereby he could adjust his desires to reality, by viewing both in fiction. As a child, he had read Horatio Alger and Oliver Optic. More important, he had absorbed from his parents a devotion to the ideals of success.

In the twentieth century, immigrants like West's parents gave renewed vitality to the dream of success. East European Jews in particular came from villages where economic individualism was as pervasive as social and religious cooperation, and while social and religious bonds were often severed by relocation, a commitment to free enterprise persisted in the new land, the Promised Land.[2] A popular guidebook advised the immigrant in terms drawn, like West's novel, directly from Horatio Alger: "Hold fast, this is most necessary in America. Forget your past, your customs and your ideals. Select a goal and pursue it with all your might. . . . You will experience a bad time but sooner or later you will achieve your goal. . . . A bit of advice for you: Do not take a moment's rest. Run, do, work and keep your own good in mind." [3] Perhaps, as some contemporary Jewish commentators suggested, Puritanism was but a version of Old Testament teaching suited to America. In any event, West's family was saying in all its actions and in its hopes for the children what one of the heroes of Mike Gold's *Jews Without Money* shouts: "I will work alone. I will show you . . . how a man makes his fortune in America! Look at Nathan Straus! Look at Otto Kahn! They peddled shoe laces when they first came here!" [4] The American Dream was the immigrant's faith.

That faith, moreover, had been apparent at De Witt Clinton and

[1] Quotes in Leonard Feinberg, *The Satirist* (New York: Citadel, 1965), pp. 175–6.
[2] Moses Rischin, *The Promised City: New York's Jews 1870–1914* (Cambridge, Mass.: Harvard University Press, 1962), p. 175.
[3] *Ibid.*, p. 75.
[4] Michael Gold, *Jews Without Money* (New York: Liveright, 1930), pp. 109–10.

at Brown. "John D. Rockefeller would give a cool million to have
a stomach like yours," the epigraph and source of the title of West's
third novel, was an "old saying" at Brown and satirized one of the
college's most illustrious graduates, who had subsequently chosen a
Baptist minister, William H. P. Faunce, to be president of Brown.
Three times each week, at 8:30 a.m., West and his classmates were
required to gather in the college chapel to hear Dr. Faunce preach,
in mellifluous tones, the gospels and evangels of success.[5] While West
was a Brown undergraduate, Rockefeller himself had written a letter
to the students, declaring: "I believe that the Golden Rule is the
best principle upon which to conduct a permanently successful business, and that its application offers the only real solution to the problem of capital and labor." Such platitudes seemed confirmed by plenty.
In the golden glow of the twenties, businessmen rode a wave of confidence, made of high tariffs, decreases in tax on upper-bracket
incomes, easy corporate regulations, and a favorable share of international markets. Calvin Coolidge of Plymouth, Vermont—the acknowledged model for West's Shagpoke Whipple—put the assumptions of
these men into secular creeds like "What we need is thrift and industry," "Let everybody keep at work," "The man who builds a fac-
tory builds a temple. The man who works there worships there."
These were all nicely summed up in Coolidge's classic remark: "The
business of America is business." [6] Not long after the announcement of
this dogma, West's father, then millions of others, were put out of
business altogether. What, they all asked, was the business of America
now? Even while he was writing *A Cool Million*, his mother, who
periodically lived with him in Erwinna, was still harping upon the
virtues of success and encouraging him to go back to his job at the
hotel or to take up some serious occupation. She had been disappointed in his writing from the beginning. When he had given her a
copy of *Balso Snell*, she had complained that now, after telling all her
friends that she had a son who went to Paris to write a book, she
couldn't even show it to them, "because all it says is 'stink, stink,
stink.' " She thought his books were "dirty." Well, that was the gap
between generations, West had remarked lightly to I. J. Kapstein. But
in the fall of 1933, he was more concerned and asked Josephine Herbst
to talk to her about the life of a writer and the function of literature.

[5] Quentin Reynolds, *By Quentin Reynolds* (New York: McGraw-Hill Book Co.,
Inc., 1963), p. 44.
[6] Quoted in David K. Adams, *America in the Twentieth Century* (London: Cambridge University Press, 1967), pp. 243–44.

Although he was determined not to go back to the hotel, he told Miss Herbst, his family was putting pressure upon him to do so. Perhaps she would convince his mother that important critics respected his work? She tried, and Mrs. Weinstein listened silently. Then she said, "How's he going to make a living?" "It doesn't matter," Josephine Herbst said, ". . . he has to have a chance." Mrs. Weinstein repeated, "How's he going to make a living?" She loved him, but she didn't recognize his qualities. In her eyes, he had been far from a success except in the brief period of scriptwriting, when his salary had seemed enormous. In his own eyes, he made clear in letters and remarks to friends, he was like the hero of James's story "The Next Time," fated to produce one shameless masterpiece after another and yet go unrewarded and unrecognized.

West himself had early and absolutely rebelled against success ideals, of course; and he had later seen his father prematurely aged and sickened by overwork. One of the essential facts behind the bitterness of the new novel was his helpless despair over his father's death from bronchiectasis in June 1932. Edmund Wilson recorded West's feeling in his journal:

> Nathaniel West (Weinstein): Father a building contractor—died in the tool house in spite of the fact his heart was weak and the family had tried to persuade him not to go to work—gave him half-Hebrew half-English service at funeral church, up on Riverside Drive—West was horrified when he found that they had rouged the old man's cheeks and cut off his shaggy eyebrows and put a great big white tie on him. He couldn't see that there was much in the funeral service that could comfort you very much. The first spadeful of earth that he had to throw down on the coffin gave him an awful jolt.
> *"From shirtsleeves to shirtsleeves in one generation."*
> *"In this business you've got to know the value of $1.49."*

West himself wrote to William Carlos Williams just after his father's death: "I've been heartsick since. He was building an extension to the Fordham hospital in the Bronx—and although sick for the last two years seemed pretty fair lately—when he dropped dead on the job."

Still, however he rebelled, whatever his bitterness, West could never entirely rid himself of an itching desire for success and certainly never from love of the fruits of success. Now the popular failure of his previous book, *Miss Lonelyhearts,* and the desperate situation of the Bucks County farmers raised again the issue of success so meaningful for West.

In 1933 and 1934, West headed his letters "Ottsville, Bucks County." In choosing to have the mock hero of *A Cool Million*, Lemuel Pitkin, begin his career in Ottsville, West showed that he identified himself with his dismantled hero. Lemuel takes a room at the Warford House, the Frenchtown hotel where West completed *Miss Lonelyhearts*. One of the prostitutes in Wu Fong's all-American brothel is the fictitious Lena Haubengrauber from Perkiomen Creek, Bucks County, Pennsylvania. Lemuel's failure was an analogue for West's own, his way of viewing himself from the outside and so reducing the tensions to which the idea of success subjected him.

Even as West wrote, hurrying his third novel along, the papers daily brought him confirmations thaat his own involvement with success and failure was the central issue of his time. America itself, like West's comic hero, seemed to be in the process of dismantlement. The revulsion against business practices that inevitably accompanied the Depression, moreover, was intensified by the Senate banking and currency investigation, whose counsel, Ferdinand Pecora, began early in 1933 to lay bare the diseased tissue of commercial corruption.[7] While West's earliest plans for *A Cool Million* were taking shape, one after another the Lords of Creation testified revealingly to their public irresponsibility and private greed. Pecora put on a sensational national show in which he proved, as he later said, that the Stock Exchange "was in reality neither more nor less than a glorified gambling casino where the odds were weighed heavily against the eager outsiders."[8] These disclosures concerning capitalism and its folklore were striking and provided an important background to West's book. The effects on public opinion were immediate. Floyd Olson, fiery governor of Minnesota, declared that if the traditional American system, the code of Alger and Coolidge, could not prevent depressions, then "the present system of government [should] go right down to hell."[9] But in what direction would the government go? How would the shattered, dismantled nation be pieced together? Who would direct its mending? And what principles would be its cement? Everywhere, people felt a change coming. Had not a group of New York rabbis, in April 1930, announce their confidence that a new Moses was soon to appear?[10]

---

[7] Frederick Lewis Allen, *Since Yesterday* (New York and London: Harper, 1940), p. 168.

[8] Ferdinand Pecora, *Wall Street Under Oath* (New York: Simon and Schuster, 1939), p. 263.

[9] *Time*, 23 (April 16, 1933): 18.

[10] Gurko, *The Angry Decade* (New York: Dodd, Mead, 1947), p. 41.

Did not some New Dealers, Berle and Wallace among others, believe in the Social Gospel hope of a kingdom of God on earth?[11] Had not Father Coughlin excoriated Mellon, Morgan, Meyer, and Mills as the "Four Horsemen of the Apocalypse"? Perhaps an apocalypse was at hand. But what would be avenged? And what millennium would it issue in?

Floyd Olson believed he knew. In November 1933, as West was completing a draft of his novel, Olson told a convention of the Farmer-Labor Party that the true aim of radicalism was "a cooperative commonwealth."[12] West's Communist friends in New York believed that they too knew and prepared poems, essays, and fiction meant to accelerate the coming dictatorship of the proletariat. The New Dealers believed that they knew, and through the NRA and similar organizations sought to regulate individual enterprise. Indeed, instead of speaking of individuals, they referred to "each individual sub-man,"[13] regarding the individual as useful "not for his uniqueness, but for his ability to lose himself in the mass." The credit system devised by Major Douglas, proposals for huge bond issues and public works, for "hot money" which would decline in value if not spent, for work-sharing schemes—these all piled up in congressmen's baskets and editors' desks. Shortly after taking office, Roosevelt told reporters, "There are about 350 plans here in Washington, public and private. I should say that they are still coming in at the rate of twenty-five or thirty a day."[14] On all sides people agreed that individual effort was as outmoded as the antiques which Henry Ford was now fervently collecting from every dusty nook and cranny of the country.

West ended his novel with an apocalypse of a very different sort. He remembered what most of his contemporaries had forgotten: that myth is more important—since it goes deeper into the emotions—than belief, and that in a contest between traditional and radical ideals, the former would prevail. Alger, he believed, not only was the "Bulfinch of American fable" but also would be the guide to change, if change was to occur—"the Marx of the American Revolution." Perhaps it was symptomatic that Ford, like one of the characters in *A Cool Million,* was hunting antiques. In a time which critically threatened their tradi-

[11] William Leuchtenburg, *Franklin D. Roosevelt and the New Deal* (New York: Harper & Row, 1963), pp. 33, 347.
[12] *Ibid.,* pp. 95–96.
[13] *Ibid.,* p. 340.
[14] E. David Cronon, *Twentieth Century America* (Homewood, Ill.: Dorsey, 1965), pp. 218–19.

tions, Americans were more likely to revert to antique ideals than to overthrow them.

The revolution, then, West believed, would be by and for the middle classes—what his radical friends called, sneeringly, a Fascist revolution. Shagpoke Whipple, a kind of nightmarish excrescence of the bourgeois clichés of the American Dream, was West's symbol for what that dream implied. The phantom world of Ottsville and Rat River over which Shagpoke presides includes meaningless proverbs, outworn symbols, vain oratory, usury, and perfidy—and he is determined to keep these at the heart of American life. Its enemies, in Shagpoke's view of history, are the international Jewish bankers on the one hand and the Communists on the other; both oppose "the American spirit . . . of fair play and competition," and in this satiric novel both cooperate to destroy the middle-class way of life. The Depression is only "an un-American conspiracy."

However comic they seem, such appeals could have deadly serious consequences. Had not Adolf Hitler, at first regarded as a clown, succeeded in becoming the dictator of Germany by playing upon similar emotions there? Alger's books, West saw, have much in common with *Mein Kampf*; he modeled his own novel upon both. Shagpoke, who upholds for "American citizens their inalienable birthright; the right to sell their labor and their children's labor without restrictions as to either price or hours," decides to found the National Revolutionary Party, popularly known as the "Leather Shirts," whose uniform is a coonskin cap, a deerskin shirt, a pair of moccasins, and a squirrel rifle. His party will be made up, as he puts it, from "the revolutionary middle-class." Shagpoke takes the field against the combined forces of the Communists (whose officers are West Point graduates), the I.J.B. (International Jewish Bankers), and the Indians, agitated by both groups. He begins by fomenting wild riots in the South ("The heads of Negroes were paraded on poles. A Jewish drummer was nailed to the door of his hotel room. The housekeeper of the local Catholic priest was raped"), then triumphs elsewhere, and ultimately demands a dictatorship. Finally, Lem, his dupe, completely dismantled, an American Horst Wessel, is assassinated and becomes a martyr in the triumph of Whipple's forces. At the end of the tale, this "American Boy" has fulfilled his dream of success, since "through his martyrdom the National Revolutionary Party triumphed, and by that triumph this country was delivered from sophistication, Marxism and International Capitalism."

Although on the jacket of the first edition of *A Cool Million* West

accurately declared that his novel "was written without malice," nonetheless it did raise serious political issues in ways that continue to be
relevant. West was concerned with the exploitation of the individual
American under unrestrained free enterprise, as well as with the ways
in which propagandists and publicists had manipulated patriotism to
conceal this danger. In *Miss Lonelyhearts* he had written of desperate
cries for faith and belief; here, he wrote of the American faith, and of
its perversions and perverters. In the fall of 1933, he told the butcher
in the American Store in Frenchtown: "You're going to see a lot of
trouble. We're going to get into a big war, sure as hell, you can bank
on it." He "didn't believe in making predictions," he said, but he was
"sure of this: the social and psychological conditions were exactly
right for it." While it was undoubtedly true that West personally
feared and despised the Fascist disease, and was well informed on the
subject of European and native Fascism, still he could regard its
increase clinically and, in fiction, with comic objectivity.

More shrewdly than most of the social prophets of his time, West
saw the sudden, surprising upsurge of native Fascist movements as a
genuine folk movement which had connections, however distant and
indistinct, with fraternal societies, clubs, evangelical religions, patriotic symbols, and the scarcely suppressed American love of authority,
tradition, and ceremony. West saw that a time when only a handful
of intellectuals voted the Communist or Socialist ticket but hundreds
of thousands belonged to what were being called Fascist organizations
was rich in wishful thinking. The American way of dreaming took
form in such organizations. Americans treated Fascism as one more
half-comforting fantasy which offered hopes of ordered security, not
scripts for revolution. Plans of all kinds were a major form of mental
activity in the thirties, the most hurried and hasty decade of intellectual restlessness in our history. To list the semi-Fascist versions of
social security is to catalogue the sometimes comic but always desperate
and hopeful utopias of the day, most of which made their first appearances just before the publication of *A Cool Million.*

There was the venerable Ku Klux Klan, by this time generally dis-
credited, but still representing—as its leader in the twenties, Hiram
Wesley Evans, put it—"the great mass of Americans of the old pioneer
stock," who "have broken away from the fetters of the false ideals and
philanthropy which put aliens ahead of their own children and their
own race." [15] Like Shagpoke's, the Klan's slogan was "Native, white,

[15] Hiram Wesley Evans, "The Imperial Wizard Defends the Klan," *North American
Review* (1926), pp. 33–63.

Protestant supremacy." By the thirties the Klan had spawned organizations[16] like the Black Legion of Michigan (active from about 1932 to 1936), the White Legion of Alabama, the Nationalists of Texas, and the Vigilantes of California, all terrorist clubs with avowed intentions to fight Communists, Catholics, Jews, and Negroes. The Knights of the White Camellia were revived under the leadership of George E. Deatherage. Fiery preachers of social doom like Gerard B. Winrod of Kansas and Gerald L. K. Smith of Louisiana ("the greatest rabble-rouser . . . since Apostolic times," Mencken said) stumped the backwoods, and later the cities, with gospels of suspicion, and with enemies inherited from the Klan. In New York, New Jersey, and the Middle West, organizations like the Friends of the New Germany and the Amerikadeutscher Volksbund (complete with uniforms, dues, and ceremonies) ultimately multiplied into a series of uniformed groups —the Gray Shirts (or "The Pioneer Home Protective Association," incorporated in 1932), the White Shirts ("Crusaders for Economic Liberty," 1931), the Khaki Shirts (1932), the Gold Shirts, the American White Guard, the Order of '76, Father Coxey's Blue Shirts, the Brown Shirts, and the Black Shirts.

The largest and most fantasy-ridden of the organizations uniformed on the Nazi model was William Dudley Pelley's Silver Shirts. Pelley had been a scenario writer for Lon Chaney, Tom Mix, and Hoot Gibson movie thrillers, as well as a popular writer of fiction for such magazines as *Redbook, The American, Collier's,* and *Good Housekeeping.* He put this experience to work in creating the myth of the founding of his Silver Legion. One night in April 1928, according to his own account in 1933, Pelley died for seven minutes, during which he learned, from "The Oracle," of the international Jewish conspiracy and of his own mission to return America to Americans in the form of a giant corporation, with Pelley as president and all "100 per cent Americans" as stockholders, each receiving $12.50 per month in dividends. Moreover, The Oracle told him, "when a certain young house-painter comes to the head of the German people, then do you take that as your time symbol for bringing the work of the Christian

[16] In my account of semi-Fascist organizations, I refer to Ernest Sutherland Bates and Alan Williams, *American Hurly-Burly* (New York: R. M. McBride and Co., 1937), p. 255; Travis Hoke, *Shirts* (New York: American Civil Liberties Union, 1940), pp. 64–5; Dumas Malone, *War and Troubled Peace* (New York: Appleton-Century-Crofts, 1965), p. 271; Louis M. Hacker and Helene Zahler, *United States in the Twentieth Century* (New York: Appleton-Century-Crofts, 1952), p. 360; Mencken quoted in Leuchtenburg, *F.D.R.,* p. 98; Hoke, pp. 5, 24, 25; Lavine, pp. 171–178; 205–8; Hoke, pp. 7–12.

Militia into the open." After reading of the appointment of Hitler to the Chancellorship of Germany on January 30, 1933, he announced, "Tomorrow, we launch the Silver Shirts!" Spreading rapidly, the organization soon numbered as many as 75,000 members in forty-six of the forty-eight states. As in all such groups, the uniform (costing $10) was vivid and ceremonial—silver shirts, blue corduroy knickers, with gold stockings or puttees.

There would be more than a little of Pelley in Shagpoke Whipple. Like Shagpoke, Pelley made appeals to Indians—he saw subversive influences at work on them—and he recruited a redskin branch of his legion to stamp out Communism on the reservations. Although his appeal, like Shagpoke's, was patriotic and racial, still it had the same seething background of evangelical mysticism, endocrinology, radio therapy, evolution, astrology, and myth. Like Shagpoke, Pelly had affiliations to avowed Nazi groups, such as the Order of '76 and the Friends of New Germany. "If you are a weakling, or given to compromise, sentimentality, and docile acquiescence to intimidation," Pelley wrote, "you are not wanted in the Silver Legion. . . . But if you are . . . not afraid to risk your life and limb for your country, you are asked to take the Oath of Consecration upon you and step out as a True Christian Soldier, garbed in a shirt of Silver, with the great scarlet 'L' emblazoned on your banner and over your heart, standing for Love, Loyalty, and Liberation."

Observing movements like the Silver Shirts, a European visitor commented that Americans "move in a world of illusion of which, outside the lunatic asylums, there is no longer the faintest trace in Europe," where the dangers of Fascism were apparent.[17] In *A Cool Million* West wrote a novel dramatizing that lunatic world—presenting it in a solemn, innocent way, until its nightmarish horror and comedy all at once break through the appearance of sanity. Beginning in the familiar American scene, the reader is abruptly plunged into the suddenly strange American dream world, hissing and writhing with absurd hates and fears, both grotesque and hilarious. West sent his "All-American Boy," successor to Balso Snell and Miss Lonelyhearts, to encounter a new set of dissolving faiths.

West's problem in the composition of *A Cool Million* was to find or invent a literary form mirroring the character and structure of this wish-fulfillment thinking. Quite consciously, he set out to gather the

[17] Odette Kahn, quoted in Halford E. Luccock, *American Mirror* (New York: The Macmillan Co., 1940), pp. 20–21.

clichés of success literature together in a comic, ironic plot. Though the result would be far from naturalistic, naturalist-like he explored the wilderness of American myth, notebook in hand, to record the strange specimens there. Before departing for Hollywood, he had consulted with his friends about "success" books. Charles Pearce had given him some information about collections of American schoolbooks, and on his way to the Coast, West stopped in Chicago to see the schoolbook exhibition at the Century of Progress Exposition. Josephine Herbst loaned him her copy of Horatio Alger's *Andy Grant's Pluck,* and on his own he found *Tom Temple's Career, Erie Train Boy,* and other Alger books. S. J. Perelman's influence upon West's method is obvious, of course. Perelman says of himself: "I . . . became a great reader as soon as I was able to appreciate the beauty of Horatio Alger and Oliver Optic." His own use of such books as vehicles for satire in his "Cloudland Revisited" series suggests the parallel lines along which his and West's imaginations might work. West also read more recent books that appeared either to satirize success stories or to be genuine recent examples of the traditional theme, like Abraham Cahan's *The Rise of David Levinsky.* He made notes on the pronouncements by the two recent Republican Presidents concerning success, as well as those by John D. Rockefeller, Sr., and the other "Robber Barons," as Matthew Josephson was then naming them.

"These fragments I have shored against my ruins," T. S. Eliot had written at the end of *The Waste Land,* suggesting that in his ability to gather and unify in his consciousness fragments of universal wisdom, he (or his hero) had seen shards of permanent value in what had appeared to be ruin. West made his novel out of fragments of the success story.[18] *A Cool Million* is literally constructed of altered and purposefully arranged fragments of his reading in Alger and the others. In effect, he made a prose, American *Waste Land*—one, like that poem, which is composed of fragments of knowledge and belief. But in West's book the source of the fragments is hardly the wisdom of the Gospels, the prophets, or the Orient—only of Horatio Alger, Calvin Coolidge, and similar savants. And in the thirties, their "wisdom" was no longer strong enough to shore against the ruins of history. Eliot's poem has coherence because Eliot believed that there was useful wisdom in all the areas of belief called forth by his sensibility. West, on the contrary, brilliantly contrived his book to fall back at last into the useless fragments of which it is made. As the morality, advice, and situations

---

[18] I am indebted to the article by Douglas H. Shepard, "Nathanael West Rewrites Horatio Alger, Jr.," *Satire Newsletter* 3, no. 1 (Fall 1965): 13–28.

of American success stories are tested, from episode to episode, by confrontations with the facts of the thirties, the book crashes into glittering fragments—of dream, hope, and illusion. West's Waste Land is truly, finally, and unutterably sterile. *A Cool Million* is ostensibly, as S. J. Perelman, to whom it was dedicated, has said, the most comic of West's books; but with *Candide, Gulliver's Travels,* and *Penguin Island,* it belongs to the tradition of tragicomedies, since at its core lies bitterness and disillusion. Hart Crane, in *The Bridge,* and Van Wyck Brooks, in his literary histories, were finding what they believed to be a "usable past" in American myth; but West found only deceit in the past. "Only a man who had been hurt deeply," as one of West's friends says, "could write so comically."

For the narrator of *A Cool Million* West created a conventional-minded youth who shows an air of patient wonder before the monstrous. A descendant of Swift's, this Lemuel Gullible still believes in the sham of success. While the tale in general seems to be predominantly narrated from an omniscient point of view, a personified speaker ("It might interest the reader to know . . .") frequently appears, to remind us that the "mind" that could accept and relate the details of this story has entirely lost the ability to recognize the absurd and ironic gulf lying between the words of success—Alger's dream words—and the realities of the thirties imbedded in West's plot. But West's surface realism, on close inspection, is cracked and riddled by the incongruous and bizarre; for, though appearing to have committed himself to observation of a deadpan surface, West lets comic jokes explode through it and tear it apart. He had been reading Kafka as he was completing *Miss Lonelyhearts,* and Kafka continued to influence him. Lemuel Pitkin is an American Joseph K., so innocent he cannot know he is condemned. All the daily news of the thirties is in his book, the dreams of his time; but we fall through them from moment to moment into the cosmos of nightmare. What begins as observational at once becomes imaginative truth.

Like Balso Snell, Lemuel Pitkin walks through a dream landscape in which strange, ridiculous characters appear without reason or consequence, seeming to have common identities but ever taking on new shapes; where the apparent logic is nightmarish, the action is inexplicable except by dream standards. The speech on horses by Sylvanus Snodgrasse and the description of the "Chamber of American Horrors" suggest that if the focus of West's satire has narrowed from Western civilization (the Trojan horse) to American society ("in the center . . . was a gigantic hemorrhoid . . . lit from within by electric lights"), it has gained in intensity. Both *Balso* and *A Cool Million* share the savage quality of reversal possible in dreams. Both take place almost entirely in the dark. Lemuel, in summing up his insane experiences, remarks, "It all seems like a dream to me," and thus strikes at the central theme of the book, that the American dream is a monstrous nightmare.

The comic absurdity of the dreams of modern man, then, provides the source of humor in West's third book. He made no claim that he was saying something politically new. Although his novel preceded Sinclair Lewis's *It Can't Happen Here* by a year, it was by no means the earliest warning of the possibility of Fascism in America. West was attempting to be neither a Party man nor a prophet. He was writing humorously and freely in well-defined traditions of satire. When he discussed the book with his friends, he spoke about its comedy, its technique, of the comic usefulness and irony of dealing with an "inverted fable," but never of his book as a tract for the times.

Herman Melville wrote in *Pierre* that "in the hour of unusual affliction, minds of a certain temperament find a strange, hysterical relief in a wild, perverse humorousness, the more alluring from its entire unsuitableness to the occasion." West's particular kind of joking in *A Cool Million* combined his reading in satiric traditions with the brutal comedy of American burlesque. With Robert Coates, an aficionado of vaudeville, West had frequently gone to Harlem nightclubs, to burlesque, or to performances of Jimmy Durante (of whom he gave a fair imitation); and of course he had attended carefully to the Marx Brothers scripts written by Perelman. He frequently spoke of burlesque comedy as classical in form. Perhaps recollecting his college essay on Euripides, he talked to Melvin Levy in a "scholarly and accurate way" of the connection between burlesque and Greek comedy; he knew the standard routines and traced them to *The Birds* and other plays. He even knew some performers, and took Levy backstage at the Los Angeles Follies Burlesque to introduce him to the comics. Combining his native, grotesque sense of the absurd with the comic techniques of vaudeville, West wrote the kind of diabolic humor that Melville described.

In addition to the basic comedy of the deadpan narrator wandering unaware in and unresponsive to a fantastic world, West exploited several other kinds of comedy in *A Cool Million*. Most obvious is the slapstick comedy of plot. Lemuel Pitkin, an innocent young man living in Ottsville, Vermont, determines to come to the city to make his fortune. He is cheated by Lawyer Slemp, who forecloses on his house; by Nathan "Shagpoke" Whipple, the aphoristic mock-Coolidge-Pelley figure, once President of the United States, but now president of the Rat River National Bank; by confidence men, and so on; deceived repeatedly on his "way to wealth." Wealth never comes, but Lem is arrested and loses his teeth; he saves a rich man from a run-away horse and loses an eye; he joins Whipple's Fascist National Revolutionary Party and is kidnapped by the Communists. Later, he is scalped by Indians. The literary analogue of this novel, Poe's "The Man That Was Used Up," makes clear that *A Cool Million* follows in the tradition of grotesque comedy, from Poe and Melville through Kafka and Gogol, rather than in the traditions of social or political satire. That Lemuel is (as the subtitle puts it) "dismantled" rather than "dismembered" suggests the inhuman, mechanical quality of man's fate. At last, killed during the first stage of their uprising, Lemuel becomes the martyr-hero of the Leather Shirts. " 'Hail the Martyrdom in the Bijou Theatre!' . . . "All hail, the American Boy,' " Whipple's Party roars out at the end.

In the framework of this plot, West wrote several kinds of support-ing comedy. The names of all the characters, of course, are ridiculous. West also plays with the comedy of taking banality seriously. Within his overall savage reversal of expectations, he treats various forms of the comedy of reversal: the firefighters who let the house burn, the Chinese laundry-and-brothel owner who speaks Italian and was educated at Yale-in-China, the Indians who scalp instead of save Lemuel. A basic device of comedy, the sudden revelation of the dif-ference between appearance and reality, West uses again and again in situations ordinarily not comic—in particular, on each occasion when Lemuel appears to have been lucky. Each instance of luck dissolves into misfortune, a further stage in his dismantlement.

In his comedy of "the dismantling of Lemuel Pitkin" West reminds the reader that brutality has been a basic feature of American comedy. From the time that Lem is knocked off the porch steps into the cellar by Lawyer Slemp until he joins the team of Riley and Robbins near the end, Lem plays the comic victim—although, of course, West re-garded him as seriously as he did the victims in the Susan Chester letters. As Lem joins the vaudeville act, the simple-minded narrator remarks: ". . . there was much to laugh at in our hero's appearance. Instead of merely having no hair like a man prematurely bald, the grey tone of his skull showed plainly where he had been scalped by Chief Satinpenny. Then, too, his wooden leg had been carved with initials, twined hearts and other innocent insignia by mischievous boys. " 'You're a wow!' exclaimed the two comics. . . . 'You're a riot!' " The comic act they develop, emphasizing each "punch" line by beating Lem violently until he is completely dismantled, suggests that life for Lem-as-Everyman is merely a violent but comic routine, a ludicrous stage affair or tent show, the bad joke of a clichéd vaudeville act.

West begins in comedy and ends by showing that beneath the comic froth lies the bitter, salt tragedy of betrayed ideals. This is particularly true of his stylistic comedy. Obviously, characters who are trying to speak sense in a nonsensical world, to act like humans when a measure for humanity is absent, provide abundant materials for comic speech. Neither the narrator nor the characters seem to be able to relate two sentences—each utterance, in this atomistic, incoherent world, is a distinct unit. The irony resides in the reader's perception of the contradictions from statement to statement. West develops this dark comedy into the even darker suggestion that the primary use of language in modern America is deception. The novel is inhabited by confidence men and their dupes; but ultimately even the confidence men are duped by their own oratory when cunning prevails over honesty, but force and violence master cunning.

Like Lem's body and the minds of the characters, *A Cool Million,* made out of bits and pieces of Alger novels, falls into fragments. The very form of West's book is a violent, mocking reversal of the American tradition of the National Novel—John DeForest called it the "Great American Novel"—whose major practitioners had been William Dean Howells and Henry James. (While working on *A Cool Million,* West was reading James as well as Alger.) Their kind of novel was based on the amalgamation, in an American (or American-European) setting, of the widest of diversities: Howells, James, and their followers had written scores of novels—constituting a definable genre—in which Southerners, Northerners, Westerners, and Europeans meet in train stations, resorts and hotels, or great cities—novels in which, as a result of this mixing, unity is won out of conflict.

Of course, by the twenties the attempt to write this kind of novel had itself become part of the body of literary cliché. In 1923, Contact Press published William Carlos Williams's *The Great American Novel,* which Williams described as "a satire on the novel form in which a little (female) Ford car falls more or less in love with a Mack truck." In his first letter to Williams, in July 1931, West mentioned this sketch, and the idea for carrying out a full-scale reversal of the form seems to have been part of the impetus for *A Cool Million.* The celebratory tradition of the National Novel, as treated by West, is seen to be one more deception. For West, the chief images of American unity become the "Chamber of American Horrors," and "The Pageant of America, or A Curse on Columbus"; Lem takes part in both. Best of all is West's description of the brothel that has been transmuted from the famous "House of All Nations" (in Chicago as well as Paris)[19] into a brothel of American regions: "Wu Fong . . . saw that the trend was in the direction of home industry and home talent, and when the Hearst papers began their 'Buy America' campaign he decided to . . . turn his establishment into a hundred per centum American place." West's novel not only reveals the deceptions of the American dream; it is in every way a precise reversal of the very literary form in which that dream had been best expressed.

Having read widely in success literature and having followed the daily news of the stirrings of native Fascism since the spring of the year, and deciding upon the technique of piecing together, in various ironical ways, fragments from Horatio Alger, speeches by Coolidge, and pamphlets by Pelley—all altered to heighten their effect—West moved rapidly through the writing of *A Cool Million*. By early November he had finished the first, handwritten draft. In Erwinna he spoke marvelously in telling friends about his book and was clearly feeling a return of confidence. He announced to his agent Maxim Lieber that this book would be "better than 'Miss Lonelyhearts.' "

Through November he toiled with increasing confidence, and with Lieber's encouragement, on a second, typewritten draft. Harcourt was anxious to have his book on its spring list, Lieber kept telling him, and needed the manuscript by December 1; "otherwise spring publication will be out of the picture." West, as it turned out, was not able to complete the second draft by then, but he did send Lieber a typescript comprising about half the book, with an outline of the balance. Cap Pearce had agreed to make a decision on the novel quickly and Lieber hurried the materials on to him. With the money West had saved in Hollywood rapidly running out, and with his mother, now back in the city, intent that he take a regular job, he was anxious to get an advance on the royalties for his book. While he waited to hear from Pearce, he continued to work on it.

Toward the end of December there was not only snow in Erwinna,

[19] West refers directly to the Paris landmark, but in making his white slavers and Wu Fong speak Italian, he alludes also to Big Jim Colosimo's famous Chicago operation, overseen by John Torrio.

appropriate to the Christmas season, but a spell of bitter, freezing weather. During this time West, not yet finished with the second draft and by now lonely on the farm, learned that Pearce, disappointed in his novel, "felt *Miss Lonelyhearts* was one of those brilliant cries without echo, a tour de force from an author whose future looked too uncertain, etc."; that, in short, his book had been rejected. Years later, West would claim that *A Cool Million* was written as a kind of parlor amusement for his friends, and that he sent it to Harcourt, Brace only in order to fulfill the option in his contract. But such tales were only masks he assumed to cover over the bitterness he felt. At the time, West was crushed by the rejection.

Again, he would turn his pain and—for all his semblance of toughness—his considerable reservoir of self-pity, into myth and fantasy. This disappointment and his anxiety about money and his future made West later speak of his bitter desolation during this time in Erwinna. He talked of this period as if all of it had been nightmarish, and of himself as if he had been trapped and immobilized. His anguish, in any event, was vividly present to him, like a recurring, terrible dream—the dream of creative impotence and failure. He told Wells Root that the farm had been "a kind of last-ditch refuge" for him. "There wasn't anybody else around—it would be winter—and he would have nobody but his dogs and nothing to eat out of but cans and he'd be trying to write something and didn't have any future or any place to go, because his books would not sell, yet *this* was all he could do." He told another friend that in Bucks County he had lived "off the land" for a whole winter, without a dime, "poaching deer and birds and rabbits," and cutting thousands of cords of wood to keep one room, the kitchen, warm. He pictured himself as going down to the pond for water, having to break the ice, and living "like a wild, primitive Indian."

These fantasies reflect West's sense of desolation and abandonment, his fears of poverty, and his almost absolute loneliness. All these he summed up in the final detail of the story he told Root—"one of the most tragic comments on loneliness I've ever heard," Root says. "He would be so lonely in the winter down there," West told him with a kind of sad, puzzled, and wistful irony, "that he'd dance with his dogs. He didn't feel sorry for himself—he spoke of this only as an example of the dreadful, lonely, pent-up life he led, when a human being got to the spot that he was eating out of cans and dancing with his dogs."

Most of these stories, of course, were not literally true. Josephine Herbst and John Herrmann were in Mexico, but West was intimate with his neighbors, the Richard Pratts, all that winter. He had no pond, only a small brook. West's re-creation of this time in fantasy reveals, rather, the hopeless anguish he was experiencing and would embody in these stories.

The snow fell fast on the Erwinna farmhouse while West worked hopelessly to finish his novel.

Bird and Bottle

by Nathanael West

Earle Haines stood in front of the saddlery store on Vine Street, Hollywood. In the window of the store was an enormous Mexican saddle covered with heavy silver ornaments. Around the saddle was a collection of torture instruments: fancy, braided quirts loaded with lead, spurs that had great, spiked wheels; heavy, double bits that needed only a few pounds pressure to dislocate the jaw of a horse. On a low shelf, running across the back of the window, was a row of boots. Some of them were black, others a pale yellow color. They all had scalloped tops and very high heels.

Every day and all day, Earle stood in front of this store. He stood stiffly, looked straight in front of him. His eyes never followed the people who passed, but remained fixed on a sign on the roof of the one-story building across the street. The sign read: "Malted Milks— Too Thick for a Straw." Regularly, twice every hour, Earle pulled a sack of tobacco and a sheaf of papers from his shirt pocket and rolled a cigarette. Then he tightened the cloth of his trousers by lifting his knee and struck a match along the underside of his thigh.

He was a little under six feet tall. The big hat he wore added another eight inches to his height and the heels of his boots still another three. His pole-like appearance was exaggerated by the narrowness of his shoulders and his complete lack of either hips or buttocks. The years he had spent in the saddle had not made him bow-legged. In fact his legs were so straight that his dungarees, bleached a pale blue, hung down without a wrinkle. They hung as though empty. They were turned up at the bottom to form very wide cuffs, and to show five inches of fancy boot. Over his left arm, neatly folded, was a dark grey jacket. His cotton shirt was navy blue with large white polka-dots, each one the size of a dime. The sleeves of his shirt were not rolled,

"Bird and Bottle" by Nathanael West. From *Pacific Weekly* 5 (November 10, 1936): 329–31. Reprinted by permission of S. J. Perelman.

but pulled up to the middle of his forearm and held there by a pair of rose-colored arm-bands.

Next to Earle was another young man. This one sat on his heels. He also wore a big hat and high-heeled boots. He, however, had on a suit of city clothes, cheap and over-styled with padded shoulders and high, pointed lapels. Close behind him was a battered paper valise that was held together by some heavy rope tied with professional-looking knots. Like Earle, he rarely moved his head, but his jaws champed continuously on a large wad of gum.

A third man sidled up to the store. He wore the same head and foot gear as the others. He spent a few minutes examining the merchandise in the window, then turned and looked across the street.

" 'Lo, boys," he said finally.

" 'Lo, Shoop," said the man next to Earle.

Shoop saw the paper valise and prodded it with the toe of his boot.

"Going someplace, Calvin?" he asked.

"Azusa," Calvin replied. "There's a rodeo."

"You going, Earle?"

"Nope," he said without turning his head. "I got a date."

Shoop considered this information for fully ten minutes before he spoke again.

"Columbia's making a new horse-opera," he said. "Ferris told me they'll use more than forty mounted-actors."

Calvin turned to Earle.

"Still got that fur vest?" he asked. "It'll cinch you a job as a sheriff."

This was a joke. Calvin and Shoop chuckled and slapped their thighs loudly. Earle paid no attention to them.

They liked to kid Earle, and tried to think of another joke.

"Ain't your old man still got some cows?" Calvin asked, winking at Shoop. "Why don't you go home?"

Shoop answered for Earle.

"He dassint. He got caught in a sheep car."

It was another joke, and a good one. Calvin and Shoop slapped their thighs. After this they became silent and immobile again. About an hour later Calvin moved, then spoke.

"There goes your girl," he said.

Faye drove by the store and pulled into the curb some fifteen feet further on. Calvin and Shoop touched the brims of their hats, but Earle did not move. He was taking his time, as befitted his manly dignity. Not until she tooted her horn loudly did he begin to move. He walked toward the Ford touring car.

" 'Lo, Honey," he said, taking off his hat.

"Hello, cowboy," Faye said, looking at him with a smile.
She thought him very handsome. He was. He had the kind of two-
dimensional face a talented child might draw with a ruler and compass. His chin was perfectly round and his large eyes were also round.
His horizontal mouth ran at right angles to his long, perpendicular
nose. The evenness of his complexion heightened his resemblance to a
mechanical drawing. His face was the same color from hair-line to
throat, as though the tan had been washed in by an expert.

"Get in," Faye said, opening the door of the Ford.

He put on his jacket, adjusting the collar and sleeves with great
care, then climbed in beside her. She started the car with a jerk. When
she got to Hollywood Boulevard she turned left. She was watching
him out of the corner of her eye and saw that he was preparing to
speak. She tried to hurry him.

"Get going, cowboy. What is it?"

"Look here, Honey. I ain't got no money for supper."

"Then we don't eat."

He considered this for a few minutes.

"Well, we got some grub at camp."

"Beans, I suppose."

"Nope."

She prodded him.

"Well, what are we going to eat?"

"Miguel and me's got some traps out."

Faye laughed angrily.

"Rat traps, huh? We're going to eat rats."

Earle laughed, but did not say anything. She waited for him to
speak, then pulled to the curb and slammed on the emergency brake.
She was very sore.

"Listen, you big, strong, silent dope, either make sense or get out of
this car."

"They're quail traps," he said apologetically.

She ignored his answer.

"Let me tell you something," she scolded—"talking to you is too
damned much like work. You wear me out."

"I didn't mean nothing, Honey. I was only funning. I wouldn't
feed you a rat."

She slammed off the brake and started the car. At Zacarias Street,
she turned into the hills. After the car had climbed steadily for about
half a mile she turned into a dirt road and followed that to its end.

Most of her anger had disappeared when she looked at him again.

He was so handsome and had such a beautiful tan. She got out of the car.

"Give me a kiss," she said.

He took his hat off politely and wrapped his long arms around her. She noticed that he closed his eyes and puckered up his lips like a little boy. But there was nothing boyish about what he did to her. Both his hand and his lips were very active.

When she had had as much as she wanted, she shoved him away. Her hands went to her hair, then she took out a compact and fixed her face.

Faye was about seventeen years old and very pretty. She had wide straight shoulders, narrow hips and long legs. Under her tight sweater, her tiny breasts showed like the twin halves of a lemon. She had no hat on. Her "platinum" hair was drawn tightly away from her face and gathered together in back by a narrow baby blue ribbon that allowed it to tumble loosely to her shoulders. The style of her coiffure had been copied from Tenniel's drawings of Alice.

Earle started along a little path that began where the dirt road ended. She followed him. They entered a canyon and began to climb.

It was Spring. Wherever weeds could find a purchase in the steep banks of the canyon they flowered in purple, blue and pale pink. Orange poppies bordered the path. Their petals were wrinkled like crepe and their leaves were heavy with talcum-like dust.

They climbed still higher until they reached another canyon. Here no flowers grew in the decomposed granite. But the bare ground and the rocks were brilliantly colored. The earth was silver with streaks of rose gray and the rocks were turquoise and lavender. Even the air was a vibrant pink.

They stopped to watch a humming bird chase a blue jay. The jay flashed by squawking with its tiny enemy on its tail like an emerald bullet. The gaudy birds seemed to burst the colored air into a thousand glittering particles.

When they gained the top of the hill, they saw below them a little green valley thick with trees. They made for it. Miguel came to meet them at the edge of the wood. He greeted Faye ceremoniously.

"Welcome, welcome, chinita."

The Mexican was short and heavily muscled. His skin was the color of milk chocolate and he had Armenian eyes. He wore a long-haired sweater—called a "gorilla" in and around Los Angeles—with nothing under it. His white duck trousers were badly soiled.

Faye followed the two men to their camp. There was a fire burning between two rocks and she sat down next to it on a broken swivel chair.

"When do we eat?" she demanded.

Miguel put a grill over the fire and started to scour a large frying pan with sand. He gave Faye a knife and some potatoes to peel.

Earle took up a burlap sack and moved off into the woods. He followed a narrow cattle path until he came to a little clearing covered with high, tufted grass. He stopped for a moment behind a scrub oak to make sure that no one was watching him.

A mocking bird sang in a nearby bush. Its song was like pebbles being dropped one by one from a height into a pool of water. Then a quail began to call, using two soft, almost guttural notes. Another quail answered and the birds talked back and forth. Their call was not like the cheerful whistle of the Eastern bobwhite. It was full of melancholy and weariness, yet marvelously sweet. Still another quail joined the duet. This one called from near the center of the clearing. It was a trapped bird, but the sound it made had no anxiety in it, only sadness, impersonal and without hope.

Earle went to the trap, a wire basket about the size of a washtub. When he stooped over, five birds ran wildly around the inner edge and threw themselves against the chicken wire. One of them, a cock had a dainty plume on his head that curled forward almost to his beak. Earle opened a little door in the top of the trap and reached in. He caught the birds one at a time and pulled their heads off before dropping them into the sack.

He started back. As he walked along, he held the sack under his left arm and plucked the birds. Their feathers fell to the ground point first, weighed down by the tiny drops of blood that trembled on the tips of their quills.

When Faye had finished the potatoes, she put them to soak in a pan of water. The sun had gone down and it was chilly. She huddled close to the fire. Miguel saw her shiver and got out a jug of tequila. They both drank deeply. Earle came along just as they were having a second shot. He dropped his sack and took the jug.

Miguel tried to show Faye how plump the birds were, but she refused to look. He took them and washed them in a pail of water, then began cutting them into quarters with a pair of heavy tin shears. Faye tried not to hear the soft click the steel made as it cut through flesh and bone.

While the meal was cooking, while they ate and afterwards, they passed the jug. Faye grew hot and excited. She smoked a lot of cigarettes.

Both men stared at her. She knew what they were thinking but seemed not to care. She assumed enticing positions and made little, obscene gestures with her tongue and hands. Miguel opened his mouth several times as though to shout, but only gulped a deep breath of air. Earle shifted uneasily on his haunches and began to curse quietly.

Faye was frightened, but her fear, instead of making her wary, made her still more reckless. She took a long pull at the jug and got up to dance. She held her skirt well above her knees and did a slow rhumba. Her round bare thighs flashed silver and rose in the half-dark. She shook her yellow head.

Miguel made music for her. He clapped his hands and sang: "Tony's wife . . ."

Earle beat out the rhythm on a box with a thick stick.

"Tony's wife . . ."

Miguel stood up to dance. He struck the soft ground heavily with his feet and circled around her. They danced back to back and bumped each other.

Earle, too, began to dance. He did a crude hoe-down, the only dance he knew. He leaped into the air, knocked his heels together and whooped. But he felt out of it. Despite the noise he made, they ignored him.

The slow beat of the rhumba went on. Faye and the Mexican retreated and advanced, came together and separated again with a precision that only the blood knows.

She saw the blow before it fell. She saw Earle raise his stick and bring it down on Miguel's head. She heard the thud and saw him go to his knees still dancing, his body reluctant to acknowledge the interruption.

There is release in running; flight, too, is of the blood. She ran up the hill, then down into the canyon, then down into the next canyon.

She sat down on a fender. In a little while her breathing became normal again and her heart stopped pounding. The violent exercise had driven most of the heat out of her blood, but there was still enough left to make her tingle pleasantly. She felt comfortably relaxed, even happy.

Somewhere in the canyon a bird began to sing. She listened to its song and sighed with pleasure. At first the low, rich music sounded like water dripping on something hollow, the bottom of a silver pot perhaps; then like a stick dragged slowly over the strings of a harp.

The bird stopped as suddenly as it had begun. She got into the Ford and drove off down the hill.

The Day of the Locust

by William Carlos Williams

This is as brilliantly written a short novel as I have ever read, a most beautiful and tenderly conceived portrait of the eternal bitch. No man could wish for a better picture. If we're to know love as it unseats the intellect, this is its excuse. But the writing is what I most admire. As I grow older I waken more and more to the understanding that good writing is always rare and I am grateful for it when it appears. Nathanael West, I salute you in heaven! Had he gone on there would have unfolded, I think, the finest prose talent of our age.

It is "the year of the locust," the year of despoliation, Hollywood, any time in the 1920's. Faye Greener is the woman. West makes of her a moving picture that is close to a work of genius, that cipher. It's what she represents and desires that distinguish her. As he takes her apart, face and spirit (but not the body, that remains whole and effective) she comes alive in his hands.

The novel consists of a series of sharply but feelingly observed incidents in the life of one Tod Hackett, a painter recently arrived, with an office on the usual "lot," a designer hired for what they can get out of him. A current Yale grad, oversized, loose jointed and with little conviction of the importance of himself or his position Tod one day "sees" a girl in an apartment house foyer and from that moment finds his life beginning to blossom.

In the course of a few months which comprise the course of the story there appear such figures as the girl herself, her broken-down second-rate ex-vaudevillian of a father, Harry Greener; Homer Simpson, a refugee from a hotel job in Indiana somewhere; Claude Estee, the well-to-do success in the business; Earle, the picture cowboy, and, finally, the Mexican. There are a few others such as the child prodigy,

"The Day of the Locust" by William Carlos Williams. From *Tomorrow* 10 (1950): 58–59. Reprinted by permission of New Directions Publishing Corporation, agents for Mrs. William Carlos Williams.

Adore, with his plucked eyebrows and mule driver of a mother, but they are less important.

We are shown a visit to Mrs. Jennings expensive bordello; told the story of Homer's precipitate leaving of his hotel job in Indiana; made present at an al fresco supper party down valley with Earle, the Mexican, Tod and Faye Greener; taken to a cockfight and the wild party that follows it and finally thrown into a huge crowd of devotees, out of control, before the "world premiere" of some movie at which Gary Cooper is to appear.

The book is unevenly written, sags in one place but picks up again at the cockfight from which point it lifts itself again to the superb pace of the first fifty pages.

I remember my mother used to say, It's not hard to do a portrait of a man, but the hardest thing is to do a portrait of a pretty woman— to take it into its parts, to avoid the fixation of "beauty." Women are always wanting to fix themselves. West's women are always rushing to the mirror, under all circumstances, locking themselves in the bathroom together for it when the necessity presses.

West takes the girls down, of their vulgarity rearranging a saint from a deformed Venus, but explicitly as only a writer can. "He tried to grab her ankles as she ran by but missed." Hardly a saint, perhaps, but infinitely desirable—a platinum blond in tight silk about her inverted heartshaped buttocks, black at her father's funeral, green at her own, always tight, or a torn waist down about the shoulders, dropping her slacks to walk from the room in black lace scanties.

She hasn't any face that amounts to anything. So you have to make one, don't you? Or with a very delicate string, silver point, gather one together. The trick is to make one up, any way you can. How would you like to see a woman coming at you with a face such as Picasso gives them? Well, don't they, all the time? Are you blind? Nathanael West somehow builds Faye Greener out of such deformity before us.

Pay attention to such writing because the time is coming fast when we shall be pushed back hard upon it. Writing may—so fast that it will take your breath away—become the most effective weapon facing disaster that we own. We had better know what it is and for what it is useful in buttressing our lives and fortunes before the deliberate liars. It's made of steel and stone and is not the "rocky cliffs" of the movie junk yard whose tatters flap in every breeze.

The Boys in the Back Room

by Edmund Wilson

These notes were first written during the autumn and early winter of 1940. Since then, several events have occurred which require a few words of postscript.

On December 21, 1940, F. Scott Fitzgerald suddenly died in Hollywood; and, the day after, Nathanael West was killed in a motor accident on the Ventura boulevard. Both men had been living on the West Coast; both had spent several years in the studios; both, at the time of their deaths, had been occupied with novels about Hollywood.

The work of Nathanael West derived from a different tradition than that of these other writers. He had been influenced by those post-war Frenchmen who had specialized, with a certain preciosity, in the delirious and diabolic fantasy that descended from Rimbaud and Lautréamont. Beginning with *The Dream Life of Balso Snell*, a not very successful exercise in this vein of phantasmagoria, he published, after many revisions, a remarkable short novel called *Miss Lonelyhearts*. This story of a newspaper hack who conducts an "advice to the lovelorn" department and eventually destroys himself by allowing himself to take too seriously the sorrows and misfortunes of his clients, had a poetic-philosophical point of view and a sense of phrase as well as of chapter that made it seem rather European than American. It was followed by *A Cool Million*, a less ambitious book, which both parodied Horatio Alger and more or less reproduced *Candide* by reversing the American success story. In his fourth book, *The Day of the Locust*, he applied his fantasy and irony to the embarrassment of rich materials offered by the movie community. I

"The Boys in the Back Room" by Edmund Wilson. From *Classics and Commercials: A Literary Chronicle of the Forties* (New York: Farrar, Straus & Giroux, Inc., 1950), pp. 51–56. Reprinted by permission of the author.

wrote a review of this novel in 1939, and I shall venture to append it here—with apologies for some repetition of ideas expressed above—to make the California story complete:

Nathanael West, the author of *Miss Lonelyhearts,* went to Hollywood a few years ago, and his silence had been causing his readers alarm lest he might have faded out on the Coast as so many of his fellows have done. But Mr. West, as this new book happily proves, is still alive beyond the mountains, and quite able to set down what he feels and sees—has still, in short, remained an artist. His new novel, *The Day of the Locust,* deals with the nondescript characters on the edges of the Hollywood studios: an old comic who sells shoe polish and his film-struck daughter; a quarrelsome dwarf; a cock-fighting Mexican; a Hollywood cowboy and a Hollywood Indian; and an undeveloped hotel clerk from Iowa, who has come to the Coast to enjoy his savings—together with a sophisticated screen-writer, who lives in a big house that is "an exact reproduction of the old Dupuy mansion near Biloxi, Mississippi." And these people have been painted as distinctly and polished up as brightly as the figures in Persian miniatures. Their speech has been distilled with a sense of the flavorsome and the characteristic which makes John O'Hara seem pedestrian, Mr. West has footed a precarious way and has not slipped at any point into relying on the Hollywood values in describing the Hollywood people. The landscapes, the architecture and the interior decoration of Beverly Hills and vicinity have been handled with equal distinction. Everyone who has ever been in Los Angeles knows how the mere aspect of things is likely to paralyze the aesthetic faculty by providing no *point d'appui* from which to exercise its discrimination, if it does not actually stun the sensory apparatus itself, so that accurate reporting becomes impossible. But Nathanael West has stalked and caught some fine specimens of these Hollywood lepidoptera and impaled them on fastidious pins. Here are Hollywood restaurants, apartment houses, funeral churches, brothels, evangelical temples and movie sets—in this latter connection, an extremely amusing episode of a man getting nightmarishly lost in the Battle of Waterloo. Mr. West's surrealist beginnings have stood him in good stead on the Coast.

The doings of these people are bizarre, but they are also sordid and senseless. Mr. West has caught the emptiness of Hollywood; and he is, as far as I know, the first writer to make this emptiness horrible. The most impressive thing in the book is his picture of the people from the Middle West who, retiring to sunlit leisure, are trying to leave behind them the meagerness of their working lives; who desire something different from what they have had but do not know what they desire, and have no other resources for amusement than gaping at movie stars and listening to Aimee McPherson's sermons. In the last episode, a crowd of these people, who have come out to see the celebrities at an opening, is set off by an insane act of violence on the part of the cretinous hotel clerk, and gives way to an outburst of mob mania. The America of the murders and rapes which fill the Los Angeles papers is only the obverse side of the America of the inanities of the movies. Such people—Mr. West seems to say—dissatisfied, yet with no ideas, no objectives and no interest in anything vital, may in the mass be capable of anything. The day dreams purveyed by Hollywood, the romances that in movie stories can be counted on to have whisked around all obstacles and adroitly knocked out all "menaces" by the time they have run off their reels, romances which their fascinated audiences have never been able to live themselves—only cheat them and embitter their frustration. Of such mobs are the followers of fascism made.

I think that the book itself suffers a little from the lack of a center in the community with which it deals. It has less concentration than *Miss Lonelyhearts.* Mr. West has introduced a young Yale man who, as an educated and healthy human being, is supposed to provide a normal point of view from which the deformities of Hollywood may be criticized; but it is also essential to the story that this young man should find himself swirling around in the same aimless eddies as the others. I am not sure that it is really possible to do anything substantial with Hollywood except by making it, as John Dos Passos did in *The Big Money,* a part of a larger picture which has its center in a larger world. But in the meantime Nathanael West has survived to write another distinguished book—in its peculiar combination of amenity of surface and felicity of form and style with ugly subject matter and somber feeling, quite unlike —as *Miss Lonelyhearts* was—the books of anyone else.

Scott Fitzgerald, who at the time of his death had published only short stories about the movies, had been working for some time on a novel [1] in which he had tackled the key figure of the industry: the successful Hollywood producer. This subject has also been attempted, with sharp observation and much humor, by Mr. Budd Schulberg, Jr.; whose novel *What Makes Sammy Run* has been published since my articles were written. But Mr. Schulberg is still a beginner, and his work in *What Makes Sammy Run* does not rise above the level of a more sincere and sensitive George Kaufman; whereas Scott Fitzgerald, an accomplished artist, had written a considerable part of what promised to be by all odds the best novel ever devoted to Hollywood. Here you are shown the society and the business of the movies, no longer through the eyes of the visitor to whom everything is glamorous or ridiculous, but from the point of view of people who have grown up or lived with the industry and to whom its values and laws are

[1] Later published as *The Last Tycoon.*

their natural habit of life. These are criticized by higher standards and in the knowledge of wider horizons, but the criticism is implicit in the story; and in the meantime, Scott Fitzgerald, by putting us inside their group and making us take things for granted, is able to excite an interest in the mixed destiny of his Jewish producer of a kind that lifts the novel quite out of the class of this specialized Hollywood fiction and relates it to the story of man in all times and all places.

Both West and Fitzgerald were writers of a conscience and with natural gifts rare enough in America or anywhere; and their failure to get the best out of their best years may certainly be laid partly to Hollywood, with its already appalling record of talent depraved and wasted.

Nathanael West's

The Day of the Locust and *Sanctuary*

by *Carvel Collins*

Nathanael West's novels are attracting more attention than formerly, and deservedly so. Now that *The Day of the Locust* is widely available in a paper-backed edition, students of Faulkner might be interested to note the use which West made of *Sanctuary* when he wrote this, his second-best-known, novel. Borrowings from Faulkner among the current French writers who concoct synthetic novels "from the American" are too familiar and inartistic to document, but West's borrowings from *Sanctuary* in *The Day of the Locust* have not been noticed and are extremely effective.

Faulkner and West first knew each other in New York in the early 'thirties when West was manager of the Hotel Sutton, where Faulkner often spent hours visiting with one of the more permanent of the hotel's guests, Dashiell Hammett, who has told me about the association of West and Faulkner and about West's admiration for Faulkner's work. I believe West showed this admiration concretely by the skillful —and entirely admirable—use he made of *Sanctuary* while conceiving and writing *The Day of the Locust*.

Faulkner's novel is set in Memphis while West's is in Hollywood, and their plots have large elements which are not in common, but both books show their authors' disgust with a degraded society. And for several elements *The Day of the Locust* seems specifically indebted to *Sanctuary*. West's wooden cowboy, Earle, has some of the characteristics of Faulkner's Popeye: Earle's face is described as being mechanically constructed by compass and ruler in a way reminiscent of Popeye's mechanical face with eyes like rubber knobs and his general look of being stamped out of tin. Earle may be a literary descendant of Faulkner's Popeye in an additional way: Popeye disgustingly killed two lovebirds, leaving beside them "the bloody scissors with which he had cut them up alive." Earle, much more normal, prepares quail as food by "cutting them into quarters with a pair of heavy tin shears." But West emphasized the unpleasantness of that operation by adding that "Faye held her hands over her ears in order not to hear the soft click made by the blades as they cut through flesh and bone."

Like Popeye, Earle is mechanical in movement, speaks little, and seethes with emotion under a calm exterior. Earle's girl, Faye, makes love with Earle's Mexican companion in a situation slightly similar to that of Popeye and Red and Temple Drake in *Sanctuary*.

Other elements in West's book seem related to Faulkner's, though somewhat less specifically. The role played by West's Tod Hackett throughout *The Day of the Locust* is similar to that of Faulkner's weak Horace Benbow in *Sanctuary*, and Hackett in his relation to Faye Greener seems similar to Benbow in his relation to Ruby Lamar. Though West possibly based his genuinely refined brothel madam on a real Hollywood woman, his inclusion of her in his novel may owe something to the presence in *Sanctuary* of Miss Reba, whose pretended refinement comically collapses in her well-known scene with the two other madams. West's unpleasantly precocious small boy, Adore, may possibly derive in part from Faulkner's precociously vicious small boy, "Uncle Bud," who takes part in that three madams episode at Miss Reba's place. Each novel contains a violent mob, overwhelming in its mindless action. And a central feature of each novel is a hide-out where the men pass each other large containers of powerful alcoholic drinks while they gather, fascinated, around a sexually attractive young girl, over whom they eventually fight.

One might even go so far as to see signs of West's borrowing from *Sanctuary* in a completely insignificant detail common to both books: West's Hollywood screen writer, the thin Claude Estee, pretending at his fake Southern mansion to be a gentleman in the Old South, imagines himself to have a paunch, which may owe part of its origin to Faulkner's description in *Sanctuary* of Temple Drake's aristocratic father with his paunch "buttoned snugly into his immaculate linen suit."

In arranging these similarities West handled himself with his usual talent and followed the artistic rule enunciated by E. E. Cummings when he said that a good artist does not borrow from another, "he steals." West repeated the theme of *Sanctuary* and so effectively integrated elements of that novel into his own that *The Day of the Locust* has no second-hand air about it whatever, with the possible exception of parts of the characterization of the cowboy Earle—and even he is vividly memorable in his own right.

These similarities are interesting, it seems to me; but one large dissimilarity also holds some interest. *Sanctuary* has been usually regarded as a shocker and a book of almost total despair. But West's novel probably is more despairing, for though he followed Faulkner in a surprising number of motifs, West chose not to follow him in presenting any character so admirable as the dignified, stoical, realistic Ruby Lamar, who gives to much of *Sanctuary* a tragic air above shock and corncob scandal.

West's Disease

by W. H. Auden

Nathanael West is not, strictly speaking, a novelist; that is to say, he does not attempt an accurate description either of the social scene or of the subjective life of the mind. For his first book, he adopted the dream convention, but neither the incidents nor the language are credible as a transcription of a real dream. For his other three, he adopted the convention of a social narrative; his characters need real food, drink and money, and live in recognizable places like New York or Hollywood, but, taken as feigned history, they are absurd. Newspapers do, certainly, have Miss Lonelyhearts columns; but in real life these are written by sensible, not very sensitive, people who conscientiously give the best advice they can, but do not take the woes of their correspondents home with them from the office, people, in fact, like Betty of whom Mr. West's hero says scornfully:

> Her world was not the world and could never include the readers of his column. Her sureness was based on the power to limit experience arbitrarily. Moreover, his confusion was significant, while her order was not.

On Mr. West's paper, the column is entrusted to a man the walls of whose room

> were bare except for an ivory Christ that hung opposite the foot of the bed. He had removed the figure from the cross to which it had been fastened and had nailed it to the walls with large spikes. . . . As a boy in his father's church, he had discovered that something stirred in him when he shouted the name of Christ, something secret and enormously powerful. He had played with this thing, but had never allowed it to come alive. He knew now what this thing was—hysteria, a snake whose

scales were tiny mirrors in which the dead world takes on a semblance of life, and how dead the world is . . . a world of doorknobs.

It is impossible to believe that such a character would ever apply for a Miss Lonelyhearts job (in the hope, apparently, of using it as a stepping-stone to a gossip column), or that, if by freak chance he did, any editor would hire him.

Again, the occupational vice of the editors one meets is an over-estimation of the social and moral value of what a newspaper does. Mr. West's editor, Shrike, is a Mephisto who spends all his time exposing to his employees the meaninglessness of journalism:

> "Miss Lonelyhearts, my friend, I advise you to give your readers stones. When they ask for bread don't give them crackers as does the Church, and don't, like the State, tell them to eat cake. Explain that man cannot live by bread alone and give them stones. Teach them to pray each morning: 'Give us this day our daily stone.' "

Such a man, surely, would not be a Feature Editor long.

A writer may concern himself with a very limited area of life and still convince us that he is describing the real world, but one becomes suspicious when, as in West's case, whatever world he claims to be describing, the dream life of a highbrow, lowbrow existence in Hollywood, or the American political scene, all these worlds share the same peculiar traits—no married couples have children, no child has more than one parent, a high percentage of the inhabitants are cripples, and the only kind of personal relation is the sado-masochistic.

There is, too, a curious resemblance among the endings of his four books.

> His body broke free of the bard. It took on a life of its own; a life that knew nothing of the poet Balso. Only to death can this release be likened—the mechanics of decay. After death the body takes command; it performs the manual of disintegration with a marvelous certainty. So now, his body performed the evolutions of love with a like sureness. In this activity, Home and Duty, Love and Art were forgotten. . . . His body screamed and shouted as it marched and uncoiled; then with one heaving shout of triumph, it fell back quiet.

> He was running to succor them with love. The cripple turned to escape, but he was too slow and Miss Lonelyhearts caught him. . . . The gun inside the package exploded and Miss Lonelyhearts fell, dragging the cripple with him. They both rolled part of the way down stairs.

"I am a clown," he began, "but there are times when even clowns must grow serious. This is such a time. I . . ." Lem got no further. A shot rang out and he fell dead, drilled through the heart by an assassin's bullet.

He was carried through the exit to the back street and lifted into a police car. The siren began to scream and at first he thought he was making the noise himself. He felt his lips with his hands. They were clamped tight. He knew then it was the siren. For some reason this made him laugh and he began to imitate the siren as loud as he could.

An orgasm, two sudden deaths by violence, a surrender to madness, are presented by West as different means for securing the same and desirable end, escape from the conscious Ego and its make-believe. Consciousness, it would seem, does not mean freedom to choose, but freedom to play a fantastic role, an unreality from which a man can only be delivered by some physical or mental explosion outside his voluntary control.

There are many admirable and extremely funny satirical passages in his books, but West is not a satirist. Satire presupposes conscience and reason as the judges between the true and the false, the moral and the immoral, to which it appeals, but for West these faculties are themselves the creators of unreality.

His books should, I think, be classified as Cautionary Tales, parables about a Kingdom of Hell whose ruler is not so much the Father of Lies as the Father of Wishes. Shakespeare gives a glimpse of this hell in *Hamlet,* and Dostoievsky has a lengthy description in *Notes from the Underground,* but they were interested in many hells and heavens Compared with them, West has the advantages and disadvantages of the specialist who knows everything about one disease and nothing about any other. He was a sophisticated and highly skilled literary craftsman, but what gives all his books such a powerful and disturbing fascination, even *A Cool Million,* which must, I think, be judged a failure, owes nothing to calculation. West's descriptions of Inferno have the authenticity of firsthand experience: he has certainly been there, and the reader has the uncomfortable feeling that his was not a short visit.

All his main characters suffer from the same spiritual disease which, in honor of the man who devoted his life to studying it, we may call West's Disease. This is a disease of consciousness which renders it incapable of converting wishes into desires. A lie is false; what it asserts is not the case. A wish is fantastic; it knows what is the case but refuses to accept it. All wishes, whatever their apparent content, have the same and unvarying meaning: "I refuse to be what I am." A wish, therefore, is either innocent and frivolous, a kind of play, or a serious expression of guilt and despair, a hatred of oneself and every being one holds responsible for oneself.

Our subconscious life is a world ruled by wish but, since it is not a world of action, this is harmless; even nightmare is playful, but it is the task of consciousness to translate wish into desire. If, for whatever reason, self-hatred or self-pity, it fails to do this, it dooms a human being to a peculiar and horrid fate. To begin with, he cannot desire anything, for the present state of the self is the ground of every desire, and that is precisely what the wisher rejects. Nor can he believe anything, for a wish is not a belief; whatever he wishes he cannot help knowing that he could have wished something else. At first he may be content with switching from one wish to another:

> She would get some music on the radio, then lie down on her bed and shut her eyes. She had a large assortment of stories to choose from. After getting herself in the right mood, she would go over them in her mind as though they were a pack of cards, discarding one after another until she found one that suited. On some days she would run through the whole pack without making a choice. When that happened, she would either go down to Fine Street for an ice-cream soda or, if she were broke, thumb over the pack again and force herself to choose.
>
> While she admitted that her method was too mechanical for the best results and that it was better to slip into a dream naturally, she said that any dream was better than none and beggars couldn't be choosers.

But in time, this ceases to amuse, and the wisher is left with the despair which is the cause of all of them:

> When not keeping house, he sat in the back yard, called the patio by the real estate agent, in a broken down deck chair. In one of the closets he had found a tattered book and he held it in his lap without looking at it. There was a much better view to be had in any direction other than the one he faced. By moving his chair in a quarter circle he could have seen a large part of the canyon twisting down to the city below. He never thought of making this shift. From where he sat, he saw the closed door of the garage and a patch of its shabby, tarpaper roof.

A sufferer from West's Disease is not selfish but absolutely self-centered. A selfish man is one who satisfies his desires at other people's expense; for this reason, he tries to see what others are really like and often sees them extremely accurately in order that he may make use of them. But, to the self-centered man, other people only exist as images either of what he is or of what he is not, his feeling towards them are projections of the pity or the hatred he feels for himself and anything he does to them is really done to himself. Hence the inconsistent and unpredictable behavior of a sufferer from West's Disease: he may kiss your feet one moment and kick you in the jaw the next and, if you were to ask him why, he could not tell you.

In its final stages, the disease reduces itself to a craving for violent physical pain—this craving, unfortunately, can be projected onto others—for only violent pain can put an end to wishing *for* something and produce the real wish of necessity, the cry "Stop!"

All West's books contain cripples. A cripple is unfortunate and his misfortune is both singular and incurable. Hunchbacks, girls without noses, dwarfs, etc., are not sufficiently common in real life to appear as members of an unfortunate class, like the very poor. Each one makes the impression of a unique case. Further, the nature of the misfortune, a physical deformity, makes the victim repellent to the senses of the typical and normal, and there is nothing the cripple or others can do to change his condition. What attitude towards his own body can he have then but hatred? As used by West, the cripple is, I believe, a symbolic projection of the state of wishful self-despair, the state of those who will not accept themselves in order to change themselves into what they would or should become, and justify their refusal by thinking that being what they are is uniquely horrible and uncurable. To look at, Faye Greener is a pretty but not remarkable girl; in the eyes of Faye Greener, she is an exceptionally hideous spirit.

In saying that cripples have this significance in West's writing, I do not mean to say that he was necessarily aware of it. Indeed, I am inclined to think he was not. I suspect that, consciously, he thought pity and compassion were the same thing, but what the behavior of his "tender" characters shows is that all pity is self-pity and that he who pities others is incapable of compassion. Ruthlessly as he exposes his dreamers, he seems to believe that the only alternative to despair is to become a crook. Wishes may be unreal, but at least they are not, like all desires, wicked:

> His friends would go on telling such stories until they were too drunk to talk. They were aware of their childishness, but did not know how else to revenge themselves. At college, and perhaps for a year afterwards, they had believed in Beauty and in personal expression as an absolute end. When they lost this belief, they lost everything. Money and fame meant nothing to them. They were not worldly men.

The use of the word *worldly* is significant. West comes very near to accepting the doctrine of the Marquis de Sade—there are many resemblances between *A Cool Million* and *Justine*—to believing, that is, that the creation is essentially evil and that goodness is contrary to its laws, but his moral sense revolted against Sade's logical conclusion that it was therefore a man's duty to be as evil as possible. All West's "worldly" characters are bad men, most of them grotesquely bad, but here again his artistic instinct seems at times to contradict his conscious intentions. I do not think, for example, that he meant to make Wu Fong, the brothel-keeper, more sympathetic and worthy of respect than, say, Miss Lonelyhearts or Homer Simpson, but that is what he does:

> Wu Fong was a very shrewd man and a student of fashion. He saw that the trend was in the direction of home industry and home talent and when the Hearst papers began their "Buy American" campaign, he decided to get rid of all the foreigners in his employ and turn his establishment into a hundred percentum American place. He engaged Mr. Asa Goldstein to redecorate the house and that worthy designed a Pennsylvania Dutch, Old South, Log Cabin Pioneer, Victorian New York, Western Cattle Days, Californian Monterey, Indian and Modern Girl series of interiors. . . .
>
> He was as painstaking as a great artist and in order to be consistent as one he did away with the French cuisine and wines traditional to his business. Instead, he substituted an American kitchen and cellar. When a client visited Lena Haubengruber, it was possible for to eat roast groundhog and drink Sam Thompson rye. While with Alice Sweethorne, he was served sow belly with grits and bourbon. In Mary Judkins' rooms he received, if he so desired, fried squirrel and corn liquor. In the suite occupied by Patricia Van Riis, lobster and champagne were the rule. The patrons of Powder River Rose usually ordered mountain oysters and washed them down with forty rod. And so on down the list. . . .

After so many self-centered despairers who cry in their baths or bare their souls in barrooms, a selfish man like this, who takes pride in doing something really well, even if it is running a brothel, seems almost a good man.

There have, no doubt, always been cases of West's Disease, but the chances of infection in a democratic and mechanized society like our own are much greater than in the more static and poorer societies of earlier times.

When, for most people, their work, their company, even their marriages, were determined, not by personal choice or ability, but by the class into which they were born, the individual was less tempted to develop a personal grudge against Fate; his fate was not his own but that of everyone around him.

But the greater the equality of opportunity in a society becomes, the more obvious becomes the inequality of the talent and character among individuals, and the more bitter and personal it must be to fail, particularly for those who have some talent but not enough to win them second or third place.

In societies with fewer opportunities for amusement, it was also easier to tell a mere wish from a real desire. If, in order to hear some music, a man has to wait for six months and then walk twenty miles, it is easy to tell whether the words, "I should like to hear some music," mean what they appear to mean, or merely, "At this moment I should like to forget myself." When all he has to do is press a switch, it is more difficult. He may easily come to believe that wishes can come true. This is the first symptom of West's Disease; the later symptoms are less pleasant, but nobody who has read Nathanael West can say that he wasn't warned.

Nathanael West: A Particular Kind of Joking

by Norman Podhoretz

The Complete Works of Nathanael West comprises four short novels amounting to only four hundred and twenty-one pages—West was killed in an automobile accident in 1940, at the age of thirty-seven —but it contains some of the best writing that has been produced by an American in this century. During the 30's, West earned the admiration of several important critics, and his two most impressive novels, *Miss Lonelyhearts* and *The Day of the Locust,* are still widely circulated and praised; the others, *The Dream Life of Balso Snell* and *A Cool Million,* have only now been rescued, by the publication of this collected volume, from virtual oblivion. But though West has not exactly been ignored, neither has he been given the close attention he deserves. His name seldom comes up in discussions of modern American literature, and even now it is not clearly realized that, for all the "bitterness" and "savagery" people find in his work, he was first and last a writer of comedy. A year before his death, West complained that his novels were disliked because they fell "between the different schools of writing." He considered himself, he said, on the side of the "radical press," but the radicals objected to his "particular kind of joking," and the "highbrow press" accused him of avoiding the "big, significant things." It is difficult to imagine what the "highbrows" (whoever they were) could have meant; the big, significant things are precisely what West pursued, to greater effect, in my opinion, than Fitzgerald, who lacked West's capacity for intelligent self-criticism, or even Hemingway, whose view of life seems to me rather more limited than West's. But the "radical press" was right in being disturbed by West. Nothing could be further from the spirit of his work than a faith in the power of new social arrangements or economic

"Nathanael West: A Particular Kind of Joking" by Norman Podhoretz. From *Doings and Undoings: The Fifties and After in American Writing* (New York: Farrar, Straus & Giroux, 1964), pp. 65–75. © 1957, 1964 by Norman Podhoretz. First published in the *New Yorker*. Reprinted by permission of the publisher.

systems to alleviate the misery of the human condition. West was one of the few novelists of the 30's who succeeded in generalizing the horrors of the depression into a universal image of human suffering. His "particular kind of joking" has profoundly unpolitical implications; it is a way of saying that the universe is always rigged against us and that our efforts to contend with it invariably lead to absurdity. This sort of laughter—which, paradoxically, has the most intimate connection with compassion—is rarely heard in American literature, for it is not only anti-"radical" but almost un-American in its refusal to admit the possibility of improvement, amelioration, or cure.

Yet West was also capable of lesser kinds of joking. His first novel, *The Dream Life of Balso Snell*—written mainly during a two-year stay in Paris, when he was in his early twenties, but not published until 1931—is a brilliantly insane surrealist fantasy that tries very hard to mock Western culture out of existence. Balso, who seems sometimes to represent the naïve romantic poet and sometimes the philistine American, comes upon the Trojan horse while wandering on the plains of Troy and literally gets inside Western culture by entering the horse (which is, of course, a symbol of that culture) through "the posterior opening of the alimentary canal." He meets a series of strange characters who inhabit the horse's innards, and each encounter is an occasion for West to deride art, religion, or civilization itself in the most shocking terms he can think of. There is, for example, Maloney the Areopagite, "naked except for a derby in which thorns were sticking" and "attempting to crucify himself with thumb tacks." Maloney, a mystic, is compiling a biography of St. Puce, "a flea who was born, lived, and died beneath the arm of our Lord." This trick of associating a pious idea with physical images evoking disgust is used generously throughout the novel, which overflows with references to diseased internal organs, mucus, and the like.

But it is all done much too innocently and exuberantly to be as offensive as West seemed to want it to be, and in any case the effort to *épater le bourgeois* is by no means the main purpose of *Balso Snell*. West incorporates into the novel several self-contained short stories that he obviously composed with intense seriousness. The most interesting—the confession of an insane intellectual who has murdered an idiot for what he calls purely "literary" reasons—is a precociously accomplished imitation of Dostoyevsky, and West might well have regarded its extravagant relish of the grotesque and the diseased as a form of deep spiritual insight. Instead, he attributes the story to a twelve-year-old brat named John Raskolnikov Gilson, who informs

Balso that he wrote it to seduce his eighth-grade teacher, Miss Mc-
Geeney, a great reader of Russian novels. Mocking his own work in this
fashion was West's way of telling himself that merely to indulge his
feeling for the grotesque and the diseased was morbid sentimentality,
that he had to do more with this feeling than take it at face value if he
was going to produce mature fiction. The assault on culture in *Balso
Snell* is really part of West's assault on himself; he is sneering not so
much at Western civilization as at his own ambition to become a part of
it. This novel, then, is a battleground on which West the sentimentalist
is pitted against West the cynic, each party asserting his claim to
superior wisdom and refusing to concede any value to the other.
Though the battle ends in a draw, the fighting of it must have helped
West achieve the astonishing control over his feelings that makes his
second novel, *Miss Lonelyhearts,* one of the masterpieces of modern
literature.

Miss Lonelyhearts (West never gives him any other name) is a young
newspaperman who conducts a column of advice to the unhappy and
confused. At first, his job had seemed a great joke, but after several
months—the point at which the novel begins—the letters from his
readers begin to trouble him deeply. Brooding over his inability to
help the wretched people who turn to him for advice, he decides that
love is the only answer; he must bring Christ to them. His colleagues,
and particularly the feature editor, Shrike, have a fine time ridiculing
this "Christ complex," and his fiancée, Betty, insists on driving him
out to the country to cure what she believes is an urban malaise. He
himself tries to escape from "the Christ business" through several
mechanical ventures into sex and cruelty, but the complex only gets
worse. In the end, driven almost insane by his sense of religious mission, he is murdered by one of his correspondents, a cripple whom he
had first cuckolded and then attempted to "save."

The letters are the focal point of the book, and a terrifyingly authentic expression of the misery that can be neither cured nor ex-
plained away:

> I am 15 years old and [my sister] Gracie is 13 and we live in Brooklyn.
> Gracie is deaf and dumb and biger than me but not very smart on
> account of being deaf and dumb. . . . Mother makes her play on the
> roof because we dont want her to get run over as she aint very smart.
> Last week a man come on the roof and did something dirty to her. She
> told me about it and I dont know what to do. . . . If I tell mother she
> will beat Gracie up awfull because I am the only one who loves her and
> last time when she tore her dress they loked her in the closet for 2 days

and if the boys on the blok hear about it they will say dirty things like they did on Peewee Conors sister the time she got caught in the lots.

The letters make the fact of evil a concrete presence in the novel, and it is in relation to this fact that West forces us to measure the responses of his characters. What we learn is that Miss Lonelyhearts' sentimental spiritualism is no more adequate than Shrike's intellectual cynicism or Betty's naïve unconcern; all three attitudes are equally valid and equally futile, and they constitute, for West, the three possibilities of life in a world whose one ineluctable reality is the letters. And when, in the last chapter, Miss Lonelyhearts rushes feverishly to embrace the cripple who has come to kill him but who he imagines is crying out for salvation, we realize that Miss Lonelyhearts, like Shrike and Betty, suffers in the same degree as "Desperate," "Harold S.," "Catholic-mother," "Broken-hearted," "Broad-shoulders," "Sick-of-it-all," "Disillusioned-with-tubercular-husband." That is West's profoundest joke, and it incorporates all the other jokes of the novel.

The formal perfection of *Miss Lonelyhearts*—the spareness and clarity of the style, the tight coherence of the conception, the delicate balance between opposing points of view—is an aesthetic reflection of the harmony that West had established, in the years since the completion of *Balso Snell*, between the conflicting elements of his own character. The tone never falters in *Miss Lonelyhearts*, because the strong-minded, intelligent compassion that emerged from this harmony and that was West's special and most precious quality as a writer gave him a firm perspective from which to judge experience. The impulse toward cynicism that ran wild in *Balso Snell* gets some play in Shrike, but it is now put into its proper place in a comprehensive and complex scheme of things. West regards Shrike's cynicism as a stunted form of wisdom, deriving from the recognition that all talk of salvation through love is irrelevant cant beside the reality of the letters, but he also perceives that the price of hiding behind a jeer is an inability to communicate with others—Shrike can neither give nor accept love. By contrast, Miss Lonelyhearts, the embodiment of the morbid sentimentalist in West, does have the power to reach out to others, but West knows that Miss Lonelyhearts' spiritualism also involves a failure of intelligence that drives him to foolishness and ultimately to insanity and death. And the portrait of Betty, whose refusal to be bothered by the letters leads to the frustration of her ambitions for a normal domestic life, can be understood as an assertion by West that his preoccupation with the halt and the sick is not the sign of a decadent or an immature sensibility but a necessary concern with the problem of evil.

Having accomplished that much, West had earned a vacation. *A Cool Million,* published in 1934, a year after *Miss Lonelyhearts,* seems to me the sort of venture that a novelist who has achieved confidence in his powers feels he can afford to play around with. There are many amusing things in the story of Lemuel Pitkin, who leaves Rat River, Vermont, to make his fortune in another part of the land of opportunity and is dismantled step by step, losing all his teeth, one of his eyes, a leg, even his scalp, and then winds up as the martyred saint of an American fascist movement. But this obvious satire on the Horatio Alger myth, done in mock-heroic prose, must have come right off the top of West's head. And I suspect that he may even have been trying to satisfy the prevailing left-wing *Zeitgeist,* which demanded that a novelist be explicitly political. But that was a mistake for West; what he had to say about Fascism he said much better in *The Day of the Locust,* his very unpolitical last novel.

The Day of the Locust—written while West was doing screenplays in Hollywood and published in 1939, nineteen months before his death —is a difficult book to get one's bearings in. It lumbers along at a queerly uneven pace, and one is never sure what West is up to. There is also an ambiguity in the treatment of locale and characters, both of which he portrays with meticulous regard for realistic detail while contriving to make them seem unnaturally grotesque. But once we understand that *The Day of the Locust* is intended as high comedy, and once we see that the slight touch of unreality in the narrative is West's method of trying to convey the feel of Hollywood, this apparently weird, disjointed book begins to assume meaningful shape.

A young painter, Tod Hackett, has taken a job at one of the studios as a set and costume designer. Hollywood fascinates him, but not the Hollywood of the big stars and the important producers; he is obsessed with the people on the streets who "loitered on the corners or stood with their backs to the shop windows and stared at everyone who passed. When their stare was returned, their eyes filled with hatred." The only thing Tod knows about these people is that they have "come to California to die." Later, he learns that

> All their lives they had slaved at some kind of dull, heavy labor, behind desks and counters, in the fields and at tedious machines of all sorts, saving their pennies and dreaming of the leisure that would be theirs when they had enough. Finally that day came. . . . Where else should they go but California, the land of sunshine and oranges?

Once there, they discover that sunshine isn't enough. . . . Nothing happens. They don't know what to do with their time. . . . Their boredom becomes more and more terrible. They realize that they've been tricked and burn with resentment. . . . Nothing can ever be violent enough to make taut their slack minds and bodies. They have been cheated and betrayed. They have slaved and slaved for nothing.

These living dead—together with the religious crackpots who worship in all manner of insane churches, venting their rage at the betrayal of their dreams in mad apocalytic rhetoric—are the people Tod wants to paint. He is planning a painting to be called "The Burning of Los Angeles," in which—anticipating similar fascist outbreaks throughout the country—they gather, like "a holiday crowd," to set the city afire. "He would not satirize them as Hogarth or Daumier might, nor would he pity them. He would paint their fury with respect, appreciating its awful, anarchic power and aware that they had it in them to destroy civilization." And so, indeed, West paints them in *The Day of the Locust.*

So, too, he paints the still living creatures who inhabit Hollywood. The living are tyrannized by dreams, possessed of the same "need for beauty and romance" that once animated the cheated people now waiting for death, but they have not yet acknowledged the futility of their dreams, the inexorability of their betrayal. In another of a series of pictures he calls "The Dancers," they are driven by the stares of the cheated ones "to spin crazily and leap into the air with twisted backs like hooked trout." This is a precise description of the way they look in the novel. Their bodies move uncontrollably, in jerks and spasms, as though refusing to coöperate in their struggle to achieve grace and dignity. They are "hooked" to the most elaborate, most awkward, most obvious of pretenses. Harry Greener, the broken-down old clown whose gestures all come out of an unfunny vaudeville act; his daughter Faye, who wants to be a star but whose affectations are "so completely artificial" that to be with her "was like being backstage during an amateurish, ridiculous play"; Earle Shoop, the cowboy from Arizona, who goes through life giving an unconvincing, incredibly stiff performance of the strong, silent Western hero; Abe Kusich, a pugnacious dwarf who tries to appear big and tough—these sad creatures make up the living populace of Hollywood. Tod, the artist, associates with them, implicated in their antics (he is in love with Faye), aware of their pretenses, but eager to see value and meaning in their grotesque dance of life.

West's Hollywood is a world in which the alternatives are the bitterness of a living death that is consummated in an orgy of destruction, and a convulsive reaching after nobility and grace that culminates in absurdity. There is no escape from these alternatives: Homer Simpson, the bookkeeper from the Midwest to whom nothing has ever happened, whose dreams are suppressed even in sleep, who has been reduced to a subhuman, almost vegetable condition, is finally "hooked" by the dream of love. In the last scene, Homer, maddened by the cruelty and infidelity of Faye, attacks a child who has annoyed him on the street and is mobbed by a crowd waiting outside a theater at a movie première. It is this incident which sets off a riot that finally unleashes the "awful, anarchic power" of the cheated and betrayed of Hollywood.

  The Day of the Locust was West's first attempt to explore the implications of the compassionate view of life he had arrived at in *Miss Lonelyhearts.* Gloomy as it seems, this view of life provided a sound basis for writing comedy. *Miss Lonelyhearts* and *The Day of the Locust* are comic novels, not simply because they contain funny passages but because they are about the inability of human beings to be more than human, the absurdity of the human pretense to greatness and nobility. The fact that West has enormous respect for the fury and the hunger behind these pretensions, the fact that he does not demand of people that they surrender their dreams, the fact that he responds to the pathos of their predicament—none of this compromises the comedy. "It is hard," West tells us in *The Day of the Locust,* "to laugh at the need for beauty and romance, no matter how tasteless, even horrible, the results of that need are. But it is easy to sigh. Few things are sadder than the truly monstrous." This is one of the lessons that comedy teaches—neither to laugh at the need nor to be taken in by the results. It is also the animating principle of true sympathy, which is why West's "particular kind of joking" has so deep a kinship with the particular kind of compassion that is allied to intelligence and is therefore proof against the assaults of both sentimentality and cynicism.

Late Thoughts on Nathanael West

by Daniel Aaron

West and His Contemporaries

The revival of interest in Nathanael West, now of some fifteen years' duration, continues to mount. In the reappraisal of the literary 'thirties, West has caught up with and overtaken most of the triple-decked Naturalists whose solemn and often infelicitous documentations no longer are devoured with relish. Over thirty years ago, West decided that

> Lyric novels can be written according to Poe's definition of a lyric poem. The short novel is a distinct form especially fitted for use in this country. . . . Forget the epic, the master work. In America fortunes do not accumulate, the soil does not grow, families have no history. Leave slow growth to the book reviewers, you have only time to explode. Remember William Carlos Williams' description of the pioneer women who shot their children against the wilderness like cannonballs. Do the same with your novels.

West wrote these words when, as Angel Flores observed about the same time, "the current vanguard taste" insisted "on directing literature towards the casehistory, gravymashpotato tradition," and only a few mavericks like F. Scott Fitzgerald (an admirer of *Miss Lonelyhearts*) shared West's dislike for the long-winded Scandinavian novel.

To see West, however, as a misunderstood and neglected "taker-outer" shouldered into obscurity by the more celebrated "putter-inners" is to exaggerate his singularity. Besides doing an injustice to a number of discerning critics who read his books with delight and appreciation,[1]

"Late Thoughts on Nathanael West" by Daniel Aaron. From *The Massachusetts Review* 6 (Winter–Spring, 1965): 307–16. Copyright © 1965 by *The Massachusetts Review*, Inc. Reprinted by permission of the publisher.

[1] "The entire jumble of modern society, bankrupt not only in cash but more tragically in emotion, is depicted here like a life sized engraving narrowed down to the head of a pin." (Josephine Herbst, *Contempo*, 3 [July 25, 1933], 4.)

such a view detaches him from a small but distinct group of literary kinsmen. Being a radical in the 1930's (and West was a faithful subscriber to Party manifestoes) did not necessarily mean that one had to write ritualistic proletarian novels or Whitmanesque exhortations to revolt. There was another kind of writing, Edward Dahlberg called it "implication literature," tinged with "just as deep a radical dye." West belonged to that select company of socially committed writers in the Depression decade who drew revolutionary conclusions in highly idiosyncratic and undoctrinaire ways: in the eerie episodes of Dahlberg's *Bottom Dogs* and *From Flushing to Calvary*, in the nightmarish poems of Kenneth Fearing, and in the pointed buffoonery of S. J. Perelman. Like these writers, West supported the objectives of the Left while retaining the verbal exuberance, the unplayful irony, the nocturnal surrealist fancies associated with a certain school of expatriate writing in the 'twenties.

Had West (and the same might be said of Fearing), been merely an unaffiliated rebel, an inveterate non-joiner suspicious of causes and unburdened by any social philosophy, his satire and humor would hardly have been condoned by the Communists. The 1930's was not a good time for antinomians, as the career of the brilliant E. E. Cummings attests. Orthodox Party intellectuals detected no ideological heresies in the fiction of West or the poetry of Fearing, and they never attacked them as they did a number of other literary deviationists, but neither did they regard these masters of the grotesque and the macabre as the proper models for the proletarian literature of the future. Their dark vision of society, their twisted wry comedy, their recognition of an ineradicable evil denser and more durable than the capitalist blight, violated the spirit of Socialist Realism. It was all well and good to depict the hells of bourgeois capitalism, imperialism, and fascism, but in the last reel, the glow of the Heavenly City ought to be revealed.

Literary experimentation in Left circles came more and more to be identified with cultism and individual self-indulgence. The whole point of radical satire might be lost if the writer subordinated social purpose to literary effect. When James Agee, writing in *The New Masses* in 1937, asserted that Left artists and Surrealists were both revolutionaries and "that there are no valid reasons why they should be kept apart," he was told by a Communist critic that he stood on very dangerous ground:

> Certainly the proletarian movement has made use of much that was in the early part of the century regarded as experimental. But it is the strength of proletarian art that it can take to itself only that which it

can use. Under the mandate of its approach to life and the necessity to communicate, it cannot lose itself in blind alleys. It has learned from experimental art when that experimentation actually devised effective modes of expression or rediscovered what was fine and effective in the art of remoter times. But when experimentation lapsed into cultism, the health was gone out of it.

Just what has Gertrude Stein to offer? Is not her whole attempt to divorce language from meaning a cul-de-sac? And just how will a living art, based upon realities so pressing that even former Dadaists have been forced to face them, gain from the mumbo-jumbo of the latter day transitionists?

Revolution is not made in the hazy caverns of the subconscious, not by any mystic upsurge of the human spirit. This is not to deny that the dream life of man is real; but to contemplate dream states for their own sake and isolated from the rest of reality is a sickness which we cannot afford. . . .

All who rebel are by no means revolutionary in our sense of the word. If the proletarian movement took to its bosom all who call themselves revolutionary, there would be no disciplined movement either in politics or the arts—only confusion and betrayal.

Now West could not be accused of divorcing dreams from reality, but the literary and artistic streams that fed his bizarre imagination— the French school of the *fin de siècle,* Dostoievsky, squalid pulp fiction, the comic strip, the cinema—set him apart from the Proletarians who saw no revolutionary significance in myths and dreams. For this reason, despite such discerning readers as Josephine Herbst, Edmund Wilson, Fitzgerald, William Carlos Williams, Angel Flores and others, the Movement never took West to its bosom. In misconstruing his humor and failing to explore his baleful Wasteland, it committed both a political and an aesthetic blunder.

Miss Lonelyhearts: *Variety of Religious Experience*

In "Some Notes on Miss L.," Nathanael West disclosed that his novel could be considered as a classical case history "of a priest of our time who has a religious experience." The portrait of Miss Lonelyhearts was "built on all the cases in James' *Varieties of Religious Experience* and Starbuck's *Psychology of Religion.* The psychology is theirs not mine.² . . . Chapt. I—maladjustment. Chapt. III—the need for taking symbols literally is described through a dream in which a symbol is actually fleshed. Chapt. IV—deadness and disorder; see Lives of Bunyan and Tolstoy. Chapt. VI—self-torture by conscious sinning; see life of any saint. And so on."

It would be handy if West had left an annotated copy of his William James for his biographers, and yet anyone who reads *Miss Lonelyhearts* in the light of the *Varieties* will understand what West meant when he declared that if the novelist is no longer the psychologist, psychology has provided him with a vast quantity of case histories which "can be used in the way the ancient writers used their myths. Freud is your Bullfinch; you can learn from him." Undoubtedly Freud helps as an interpreter of Miss Lonelyhearts' subliminal self, but William James, as he acknowledged, supplied the structure of the novel. West, I think, drew most heavily from two chapters: "The Religion of Healthy-Mindedness" and "The Sick Soul," but his hero displays all of the classical symptoms of the conversion experience described throughout James' book.

According to James,

> There are people for whom evil means only a maladjustment with *things*, a wrong correspondence of one's life with the environment. Such evil as this is curable, on principle at least, upon the natural plane, for merely by modifying either the self or the things, or both at once, the two terms may be made to fit, and all go merry as a marriage bell again. But there are others for whom evil is no mere relation of the subject to particular outer things, but something more radical and general, a wrongness or vice in his essential nature, which no alteration of the environment, or any significant rearrangement of the inner self, can cure, and which requires a supernatural remedy.

James hazarded the generalization (which Santayana was to elaborate in his novel, *The Last Puritan*) that it was the "Germanic races" rather than the Latin who capitalized the S in sin and conceived of it as "something ineradicably ingrained in our natural subjectivity, and never to be removed by any superficial piecemeal operation."

Miss Lonelyhearts, it will be remembered, is the son of a Baptist minister, "the New England puritan" with a high forehead, long flesh-less nose, and bony chin. He can find no consolation in the faith of the "healthy-minded" for whom evil is merely a disease and a preoccupa-

---

² Stanley Edgar Hyman (*Nathanael West*, Univ. of Minnesota Pamphlets, No. 21, p. 16) is skeptical of this claim: "some or all of this may be Westian leg-pull."

tion with evil an additional manifestation of the sickness. His "healthy-minded" sweetheart, Betty, attributes his "anhedonia" (dreariness, discouragement, dejection, disgust) to some physical ailment. "What's the matter?" she asks him. "Are you sick?" And Miss Lonelyhearts lashes back: "What a kind bitch you are. As soon as anyone acts viciously, you say he's sick. Wife torturers, rapers of small children, according to you they're all sick. No morality, only medicine. Well, I'm not sick. I don't need any of your damned aspirin. I've got a Christ complex, etc."

The conversion process is already under way. Before the unregenerate man can attain saintliness, he must go through the stages of "depression, morbid introspection, and sense of sin." Preparatory to the bliss of grace is "the pitch of unhappiness so great that all the goods of nature may be entirely forgotten," and when the sufferer happens to be a neurotic with a very low threshold of pain, his agony is almost unbearable. His anguish takes the forms of self-loathing, extreme exasperation, self-mistrust, self-despair. Miss Lonelyhearts' despair is patterned on the melancholia of Tolstoy overwhelmed by a heightened awareness of objective evil. And just as John Bunyan was sickened by the depths of his own iniquity, so Miss Lonelyhearts writhes in the presence of his own corruption and his inability to control it.

Miss Lonelyhearts' conversion during a bout of fever is quite similar to many of those recorded by William James, and although his brief interlude of ecstasy and his ridiculous death are presented almost farcically, there is no reason to conclude that West was denying the value of saintliness in his modern *Pilgrim's Progress*. The torments of the misfits and the grotesques in *Miss Lonelyhearts* may be exacerbated by sordid social conditions—it is, in a technical sense, a Depression novel—but is West really saying that the plight of Sick-of-it-all, Broken-hearted, Broad-shoulders, and Disillusioned-with-tubercular-husband could have been solved by the expropriation of the expropriators? To the healthy-minded Communist, West's lonely madman could only be judged as a dupe ministering to the duped. But the novel, as I read it, implicitly enforces rather the conclusion of William James than that of Karl Marx.

The healthy-minded, James remarks at the end of his chapter on "The Sick Soul," reject as "unmanly and diseased" the "children of wrath and cravers of a second birth." But James predicts that if the days of killing and torture ever return, "the healthy-minded would at present show themselves the less indulgent of the two." Healthy-mindedness, however adequate it is for certain cheery temperaments, fails "as a philosophical doctrine, because the evil facts which it refuses positively to account for are a genuine portion of reality, and they may after all be the best key to life's significance, and possibly the only openers of our eyes to the deepest levels of truth." *Miss Lonelyhearts* is a profane assertion of this idea.

West and Political Satire

The Horatio Alger hero in West's third novel, *A Cool Million* (1934), comes of age during the Great Depression, and after a slap-stick sequence of nasty and brutal misadventures (he loses his scalp, one eye, a leg, all of his teeth, and finally his life) he winds up as a Fascist martyr. Some of West's admirers have detected Dostoievskian profundities in his "Tattered Tom" parody, but *A Cool Million* is the most dated and the most tiresome of his novels, a sour joke that the author cannot sustain. What redeems it (besides its flashes of lurid comedy) is West's initial conception; the ruthlessly innocent American Boy, one of Norman Rockwell's wholesome caricatures, who moves dreamily through a Hieronymus Bosch landscape, survives one outrage after another and dies still loyal to his benighted code. Here is a text on the perversion of healthy-mindedness in "the days of killing and torture." [3]

A Cool Million made even less stir among the literary radicals than *Miss Lonelyhearts* did, and the reasons were not entirely aesthetic. Party intellectuals and their literary supporters tended to be as doctrinaire about the right and wrong uses of humor as they were about a good many other matters, and *A Cool Million*, through Marxist glasses, was as ideologically unfocused as its predecessor. To Kyle Crichton, "humorist" and columnist in the *New Masses* who wrote under the pen-name of Robert Forsythe, merely to have a sense of humor was not enough—especially when the working class was being slaughtered by Fascists, betrayed by Trotskyites, and deceived by the hirelings of Hearst and Morgan. Satire of the Perelman-Benchley-Donald Ogden Stewart variety, favored by the *New Yorker* magazine, merely diverted a segment of the society that was beyond redemption.

[3] West had remarked in the October, 1932 issue of *Contact*, of which he was one of the editors, that every manuscript sent to the magazine had "violence for its core." The editors, he said, "did not start with the idea of printing tales of violence. We now feel that we would be doing violence by suppressing them."

"It is the old dada stuff," Forsythe complained, "the irrelevant incongruous type of humor; you start with one thing and end up with something utterly different and silly." The purpose behind his own humor, he went on to say, was to make the working classes "realize that they had nothing to fear from their so-called betters." To Perelman, whose *New Yorker* pieces (*Strictly from Hunger,* 1937) provoked these remarks, Forsythe concluded:

> if you really want to do something with that great talent in humor, learn at what point it is necessary to stick the stiletto in and twist it around! If there is a loud scream of anguish, you will know you've written something. If it's hilarious to the people it helps, it's humor.

Forsythe's commentary makes it easier to understand why West's humor and satire were not highly esteemed in the *New Masses.* He knew how to twist the stiletto all right, but his writing also smacked of that "crazy" humor Forsythe disliked.

West had dedicated *A Cool Million* to his brother-in-law, a gesture both fraternal and literary, for Perelman, the author of "Dawn Ginsburg's Revenge" and creator of Ming Toy Epstein, was himself a master of the Victor "Tom Swift" Appleton style. Both possessed a talent for blending the esoteric, the technical, and the commonplace into absurd and brilliant combinations, and neither was at his best (despite their left-wing affiliations) when he was being studiedly political and dealing with what the Party would call "real issues." In a zany mood, Perelman could paint a dadaist portrait of the author of *Miss Lonelyhearts* that is a masterpiece of nonsense. His pieces in the *New Masses,* however, lacked the spontaneity and outrageousness of his best work,[4] perhaps because the policies of the magazine checked his

---

[4] "Thunder Over Alma Mater: The Rover Boys and the Young Radicals (*New Masses,* XVII [Dec. 17, 1935], p. 32) tells how Tom and Dick Rover and their cronies united to save old Effluvia College from "certain weak-minded members of the faculty" who "are preparing to seize power, set up a soviet in the Administration Building, and nationalize the girls of Sweetbread Hall." Master-minding this coup is Dan Baxter (really Dan Baxtrovich, "a notorious single-taxer, anarchist and firebrand." The "alert and clear-eyed" Vigilantes raid the College Library where they discover works "of a number of inflammatory and un-American writers of the crazy so-called 'modern' school. Another squad surprises a group of the younger English professors and force "the cowardly 'intelligentsia'" to recant after "some innocent horseplay involving castor-oil and a rubber-hose." Meanwhile Tom's sweetheart, Eunice Haverstraw, had been kidnapped by Baxtrovich. She is rescued just in time from her non-Aryan embraces by her husky lover who wins her hand and a managership in her father's plant. The promised sequel is 'The Rover Boys and Their Young Finks.' "

usual extravagance. They point up the dilemma of the humorist who is required to be funny about unfunny things, in this case anti-semitism, xenophobia, and lynchings.

Mr. Kenneth Burke, who has at one time or another managed to say something important about almost every literary problem, touched on this matter in one of his reviews. In 1935 Burke was serving as a superior if unappreciated aesthetician for the Marxists, and in a discussion of Kyle Crichton's humor, he extracted some significant principles from Crichton's topical and jejune commentaries.[5]

Burke defined three kinds of humorist: the "comic exorcist," the "universal satirist," and the "satiric propagandist." The first, and most acceptable to the Establishment, divert society's attentions from the portentous to the inconsequential by changing "the scale of things, turning major terrors into minor annoyances." They are much sought after by magazines like the *New Yorker,* he says, because "with the help of such magazines, the Vague Shapes of Historical Calamity are whisked away, to be displaced by odd discomforts, reassuring in their tininess." The "universal satirist" is unselectively critical, sees all mankind as foolish or swinish or worse, and is engaged in a general and universal denigration. Unlike the first two types, the "satiric propagandist" is not allowed to swivel his guns in all directions. If the "comic exorcist" hates no one and the "universal satirist" hates everyone, the "satiric propagandist" has "a clear alignment of friends and foes" and exempts the former from his wrath. He neither wishes to reduce grave problems to triviality nor to magnify them to such a degree that no solution seems possible. Selecting his targets according to a particular social platform, he sees capitalism as a system that organizes "the anti-social, giving it efficiency, voice, and authority, and consolidating it with the help of the educative, legislative, and constabulary forces."

This very selectivity, as Burke realizes, presents a danger, because the man engaged in "political excoriation," especially the self-righteous moralist, hesitates to trust his wit and humor alone. He becomes in effect an editorialist for a party and feels obliged to keep wig-wagging his message to readers whose response is partly determined by their familiarity with the ephemeral events and personalities he deals with. He dare not stray beyond the fences of their prejudices or play games with their gods, and his shuttling back and forth "between the serious

[5] "Protective Coloration," *The New Republic,* LXXXIII (July 10, 1935), 255–256, a review of *Redder Than the Rose* by Robert Forsythe (pseudonym for Kyle Crichton).

and the mock serious" is both politically and aesthetically disquieting. Into which of the Burkean categories does Nathanael West fall? Plainly he is an exorcist of a kind, for all comedy is cathartic; and clearly he tried to become on occasion a "satiric propagandist." *A Cool Million* is an anti-capitalist satire, its well-defined targets obvious in 1934 to any Communist, Fellow-traveler or even liberal. It is hardly an example, however, of the socially conscious fiction the Left-Wing was calling for, and it displays the Westian idiosyncrasies that kept him from becoming an acceptable political marksman for the Party: pessimism, an impatience with codes, and an inability to accommodate revolutionary parables to his gothic imagination.

At his most authentic, West is the "universal satirist." His humor is savage and sad, in contrast to Perelman's brash spoofing, and it springs, I think, from his tragi-comic view of the world, from his wry awareness of the disparity between secular facts and his suppressed religious ideals. His slapstick ends in a scream; the self-hatred of his characters, their efforts—sometimes grotesque and always painful— to find answers or relief, only curdles his pity. In *A Cool Million,* as in his other novels, the real culprit is not capitalism but humanity.

Chronology of Important Dates

1903	October 17	Born in New York City.
1920	June	Left DeWitt Clinton High School after three years.
1921	September	Entered Tufts College.
1922	January	Transferred to Brown University.
1923–24		Publications in *Casements* and the *Brown Jug*, college magazines.
1924	June	Graduation from Brown University.
1926–27	October 13 to early January	In Paris. Work on *The Dream Life of Balso Snell*.
1929	March	First reading of "Miss Lonelyhearts" letters.
1931	Spring	Publication of *The Dream Life of Balso Snell* (Contact Editions).
1932		Associate Editor (with William Carlos Williams) of *Contact*. Publication of early versions of *Miss Lonelyhearts*.
1933	April 8	Publication of *Miss Lonelyhearts* (Horace Liveright, Inc.).
1933	Summer	Junior writer at Columbia Studios.
1934	June 19	Publication of *A Cool Million* (Covici–Friede).
1936		Begins script-writing at Republic Studios, work that continues at this studio, R.K.O., Universal, and Columbia, until the time of West's death.
1938	November 21	Opening of *Good Hunting*, written with Joseph

Schrank. (After two performances, the play closed.)

1939   May 16   Publication of *The Day of the Locust* (Random House).

1940   April 19   West and Eileen McKenney married in Beverly Hills, California.

1940   December 22   West and Eileen killed in an automobile accident near El Centro, California.

Notes on the Editor and Contributors

JAY MARTIN, the editor of this volume, is Professor of English and Comparative Literature at the University of California, Irvine. He is the author of books on Nathanael West, Conrad Aiken, Robert Lowell, and American literature 1865–1914, and is currently preparing a biography of Henry Miller.

DANIEL AARON is Professor of English at Smith College and the author of *Writers on the Left* and *Men of Good Hope*.

W. H. AUDEN, the distinguished poet, playwright, and critic, is himself the subject of several critical books. His shorter and longer poems were collected in two volumes in 1966 and 1968.

CARVEL COLLINS, Professor of English at Notre Dame University, is the author of numerous studies of the life and work of William Faulkner.

CARTER A. DANIEL is Assistant Professor of English at Upsala College in East Orange, New Jersey.

ANGEL FLORES is the editor of anthologies of German, French, and Spanish poetry, a distinguished translator, and an authority on writers as different as Cervantes and Kafka.

DAVID D. GALLOWAY is Professor of English at Case-Western Reserve and the author of *The Absurd Hero in American Fiction*.

JOSEPHINE HERBST wrote a number of important novels, including one dealing, in part, with Nathanael West's life in Erwinna, *A Hunter of Doves*.

HANNAH JOSEPHSON recently published *Al Smith: Hero of the Cities* in collaboration with her husband and has translated the work of Louis Aragon.

S. J. PERELMAN is one of America's most brilliant comic writers and observers and was Nathanael West's brother-in-law, dramatic collaborator, and closest friend.

NORMAN PODHORETZ, editor-in-chief of *Commentary* since 1960, has written *Making It* and numerous essays on contemporary literature.

MARC L. RATNER, Chairman of the English Department, California State College, Hayward, is the author of a recent book on William Styron.

MARCUS SMITH teaches literature at the American University in Beirut.

PHILIPPE SOUPAULT, originally associated with the French surrealist movement, has written several novels and biographies.

EDMOND L. VOLPE is Chairman of the English Department at City College, New York; he has written and edited several books, including *A Reader's Guide to William Faulkner*.

WILLIAM CARLOS WILLIAMS is one of the most important and influential modern American poets. During his editorship of *Contact*, he chose West as associate editor.

EDMUND WILSON has a secure position as one of the leading literary critics in America; he has also written poetry, fiction, and history. His best known works are *Axel's Castle* and *To the Finland Station*.

Selected Bibliography

I. Books

Comerchero, Victor. *Nathanael West: The Ironic Prophet.* Syracuse: Syracuse University Press, 1964.

Hyman, Stanley Edgar. *Nathanael West.* Minneapolis, Minn.: Minnesota University Press, 1962.

Light, James F. *Nathanael West: An Interpretative Study.* Evanston, Ill.: Northwestern University Press, 1961.

Reid, Randall. *The Fiction of Nathanael West: No Redeemer, No Promised Land.* Chicago and London: University of Chicago Press, 1967.

All treat West's four novels. Comerchero sees him as a searing ironist; Hyman as a skillful and complex artist; Light in terms of his biography; and Reid as a parodist.

II. Selected Shorter Pieces

Andreach, Robert J. "Nathanael West's *Miss Lonelyhearts*: Between the Dead Pan and the Unborn Christ." *Modern Fiction Studies* 13 (Summer, 1966): 251–60. Interesting study of West's ironic use of the Pan myth.

Bittner, William, "A la recherche d'un ecrivain perdu." *Les Langues Modernes* 54 (July–August, 1960): 274–82. Argues that "the classic discovery in American letters in our time was Nathanael West."

Coates, Robert M. Introduction to *Miss Lonelyhearts.* New York: New Directions Pub. Corp., 1946, 1950. Coates was one of West's earliest appreciative critics and a close friend.

Cowley, Malcolm. *Exile's Return: A Literary Odyssey of the 1920's.* New York: The Viking Press, Inc., 1951, pp. 237–40. Puts West's major books into contexts of the 20s and 30s.

Flavin, Robert J. "Animal Imagery in the Works of Nathanael West." *Thoth* 5 (1964): 25–30. Sees the violence in West's world as basically animal.

Gehman, Richard B. Introduction to *The Day of the Locust.* New York: Bantam Books, 1953. Long a source for excerpts from unpublished letters by West.

Gilmore, Thomas B., Jr. "The Dark Night of the Cave: A Rejoinder to Kernan on *The Day of the Locust.*" *Satire Newsletter* 2 (Spring, 1965): 95–100. Argues that West is not a true satirist.

Herbst, Josephine. "Hunter of Doves," *Botteghe Oscure* 13 (1954): 310–44. A novella whose hero is modelled after West.

Hollis, C. Carroll. "Nathanael West and Surrealist Violence." *Fresco* 7 (Fall, 1957): 5–21. The best extended study of West and surrealism.

Kernan, Alvin B. "The Mob Tendency: *The Day of the Locust,*" *The Plot of Satire.* New Haven and London: Yale University Press, 1965. Relates West to traditions of satire.

Phillips, Robert S. "Fitzgerald and *The Day of the Locust.*" *Fitzgerald Newsletter,* no. 15 (Fall, 1961): 2–3. Studies West's indebtedness to *Tender Is the Night.*

Rosenfeld, Isaac. "Faulkner and Contemporaries." *Partisan Review* 18 (January–February, 1951): 106–14. The earliest attempt to define the character of West's sensibility.

Shepard, Douglas. "Nathanael West Rewrites Horatio Alger, Jr." *Satire Newsletter* 3 (1965): 13–28. With the use of many parallel passages, shows West's use of passages from Alger novels.

White, William. "Nathanael West: A Bibliography." *Studies in Bibliography* 11 (1958): 207–24; "Nathanael West: Further Bibliographical Notes." *The Serif* 2 (1965): 28–31.

TWENTIETH CENTURY VIEWS

American Authors

AUDEN, edited by Monroe K. Spears (S-TC-38)

STEPHEN CRANE, edited by Maurice Bassan (S-TC-66)

EMILY DICKINSON, edited by Richard B. Sewall (S-TC-28)

EMERSON, edited by Milton R. Konvitz and Stephen E. Whicher (S-TC-12)

FAULKNER, edited by Robert Penn Warren (S-TC-65)

F. SCOTT FITZGERALD, edited by Arthur Mizener (S-TC-27)

ROBERT FROST, edited by James M. Co (S-TC-3)

HAWTHORNE, edited by A. N. Kaul (S-TC-55)

HEMINGWAY, edited by Robert P. Weeks (S-TC-8)

HENRY JAMES, edited by Leon Edel (S-TC-34)

SINCLAIR LEWIS, edited by Mark Schorer (S-TC-6)

ROBERT LOWELL, edited by Thomas Parkinson (S-TC-79)

MELVILLE, edited by Richard Chase (S-TC-13)

ARTHUR MILLER, edited by Robert W. Corrigan (S-TC-84)

MODERN AMERICAN THEATER, edited by Alvin B. Kernan (S-TC-69)

MARIANNE MOORE, edited by Charles Tomlinson (S-TC-86)

O'NEILL, edited by John Gassner (S-TC-39)

POE, edited by Robert Regan (S-TC-63)

EZRA POUND, edited by Walter Sutton (S-TC-29)

WALLACE STEVENS, edited by Marie Borroff (S-TC-33)

THOREAU, edited by Sherman Paul (S-TC-10)

MARK TWAIN, edited by Henry Nash Smith (S-TC-30)

EDITH WHARTON, edited by Irving Howe (S-TC-20)

WHITMAN, edited by Roy Harvey Pearce (S-TC-5)

W. C. WILLIAMS, edited by J. Hillis Miller (S-TC-61)

VIRGINIA WOOLF, edited by Claire Sprague (S-TC-93)

TWENTIETH CENTURY VIEWS

European Authors

BAUDELAIRE, edited by Henri Peyre (S-TC-18)
SAMUEL BECKETT, edited by Martin Esslin (S-TC-51)
BRECHT, edited by Peter Demetz (S-TC-11)
CAMUS, edited by Germaine Brée (S-TC-1)
CERVANTES, edited by Lowrey Nelson, Jr. (S-TC-89)
CHEKHOV, edited by Robert Louis Jackson (S-TC-71)
DANTE, edited by John Freccero (S-TC-46)
DOSTOEVSKY, edited by René Wellek (S-TC-16)
EURIPIDES, edited by Erich Segal (S-TC-76)
FLAUBERT, edited by Raymond Giraud (S-TC-42)
GIDE, edited by David Littlejohn (S-TC-88)
GOETHE, edited by Victor Lange (S-TC-73)
HOMER, edited by George Steiner and Robert Fagles (S-TC-15)
IBSEN, edited by Rolf Fjelde (S-TC-52)
KAFKA, edited by Ronald Gray (S-TC-17)
LORCA, edited by Manuel Duran (S-TC-14)
MALRAUX, edited by R. W. B. Lewis (S-TC-37)
THOMAS MANN, edited by Henry Hatfield (S-TC-36)
MOLIÈRE, edited by Jacques Guichardnaud (S-TC-41)
PIRANDELLO, edited by Glauco Cambon (S-TC-67)
PROUST, edited by René Girard (S-TC-4)
SARTRE, edited by Edith Kern (S-TC-21)
SOPHOCLES, edited by Thomas Woodard (S-TC-54)
STENDHAL, edited by Victor Brombert (S-TC-7)
TOLSTOY, edited by Ralph E. Matlaw (S-TC-68)
VIRGIL, edited by Steele Commager (S-TC-62)
VOLTAIRE, edited by William F. Bottiglia (S-TC-78)

TWENTIETH CENTURY VIEWS

British Authors

JANE AUSTEN, edited by Ian Watt (S-TC-26)
THE BEOWULF POET, edited by Donald K. Fry (S-TC-82)
BLAKE, edited by Northrop Frye (S-TC-58)
THE BRONTËS, edited by Ian Gregor (S-TC-92)
BYRON, edited by Paul West (S-TC-31)
COLERIDGE, edited by Kathleen Coburn (S-TC-70)
CONRAD, edited by Marvin Mudrick (S-TC-53)
DICKENS, edited by Martin Price (S-TC-72)
JOHN DONNE, edited by Helen Gardner (S-TC-19)
DRYDEN, edited by Bernard N. Schilling (S-TC-32)
GEORGE ELIOT, edited by George R. Creeger (S-TC-90)
T. S. ELIOT, edited by Hugh Kenner (S-TC-2)
FIELDING, edited by Ronald Paulson (S-TC-9)
FORSTER, edited by Malcolm Bradbury (S-TC-59)
HARDY, edited by Albert Guérard (S-TC-25)
HOPKINS, edited by Geoffrey H. Hartman (S-TC-57)
A. E. HOUSMAN, edited by Christopher Ricks (S-TC-83)
SAMUEL JOHNSON, edited by Donald J. Greene (S-TC-48)
BEN JONSON, edited by Jonas A. Barish (S-TC-22)
KEATS, edited by Walter Jackson Bate (S-TC-43)
D. H. LAWRENCE, edited by Mark Spilka (S-TC-24)
MARLOWE, edited by Clifford Leech (S-TC-44)
ANDREW MARVELL, edited by George deF. Lord (S-TC-81)
MILTON, edited by Louis L. Martz (S-TC-60)
MODERN BRITISH DRAMATISTS, edited by John Russell Brown (S-TC-74)
RESTORATION DRAMATISTS, edited by Earl Miner (S-TC-64)
SAMUEL RICHARDSON, edited by John Carroll (S-TC-85)
SHAKESPEARE: THE COMEDIES, edited by Kenneth Muir (S-TC-47)
SHAKESPEARE: THE HISTORIES, edited by Eugene M. Waith (S-TC-45)
SHAKESPEARE: THE TRAGEDIES, edited by Alfred Harbage (S-TC-40)
G. B. SHAW, edited by R. J. Kaufmann (S-TC-50)
SHELLEY, edited by George M. Ridenour (S-TC-49)

(continued on next page)

(continued from previous page)